201 WINNING COVER LETTERS
FOR $100,000+ JOBS

Books and audios by Wendy S. Enelow:

100 Winning Resumes For $100,000+ Jobs

201 Winning Cover Letters For $100,000+ Jobs

1500 KeyWords For $100,000+ Jobs

Resume Explosion (audio)

Resume Winners From the Pros

201 WINNING COVER LETTERS FOR $100,000+ JOBS
Cover Letters That Can Change Your Life!

Wendy S. Enelow

IMPACT PUBLICATIONS
Manassas Park, VA

Library of Congress Cataloguing-in-Publication Data

Enelow, Wendy S.
    201 winning cover letters for $100,000+ jobs: cover letters that can change your life! / Wendy S. Enelow.
        p.   cm.
    ISBN 1-57023-088-9 (alk. paper)
    1. Cover letters. 2. Résumés (Employment)   I. Title.
HF5383.E477   1998   97-42388
808'.06665–dc21   CIP

For information on distribution or quantity discount rates, Telephone (703/361-7300), Fax (703/335-9486), E-mail (*impactp@impactpublications.com*), or write to: Sales Department, IMPACT PUBLICATIONS, 9104-N Manassas Drive, Manassas Park, VA 20111-5211. Distributed to the trade by National Book Network, 4720 Boston Way, Suite A, Lanham, MD 20706, Tel. 1-800-462-6420.

CONTENTS

CHAPTER 1:   Writing Winning Cover Letters   1

CHAPTER 2:   Cover Letter Samples   31

CHAPTER 1

WRITING WINNING COVER LETTERS

What Is A Cover Letter?

A well-worded, visually pleasing, grammatically correct, 100% accurate and generally one-page "marketing communication" that accompanies your resume, the cover letter is a critical tool in your job search. It allows you to highlight your skills, qualifications, competencies and achievements most related to your current career objectives.

Objective Of A Cover Letter

You have one objective in preparing your cover letter — to get an interview, phone call, fax or email communication inquiring about your experience, requesting additional information or, ideally, inviting you for a personal interview.

Critical Messages To Communicate

1. You are a top-flight candidate with precisely the qualifications and experience the hiring company is seeking.

2. The value and benefits you bring to a prospective employer.

3. Your success, accomplishments and track record of performance.

4. Your strong written communication skills.

5. Your ability to quickly assimilate into their culture and organization.

6. Your dedication and determination.

7. Your leadership and management competencies.

8. Your insight into each prospective employer's needs, expectations and objectives.

Critical Concepts To Communicate

- Success
- Problem Solving
- Performance
- Confidence

- Achievement
- Change Management
- Leadership
- Tenacity

- Action
- Quality
- Innovation
- Results

**Be dynamic, upscale and competitively distinctive in your letters.
NOT flamboyant, arrogant or boisterous.**

Cover Letter Rules & Regulations

The Five Critical Cover Letter Rules & Regulations To Live By

1. Cover letters should complement the resume; not repeat it. Do not use text, word for word, from your resume in your cover letter. Find different ways to communicate the same messages, achievements and qualifications. For instance, rather than highlighting a specific revenue achievement that is already noted in your resume, highlight cumulative revenue achievements.

2. Ask for the interview at the end of each cover letter. For example, "I look forward to meeting with you to pursue the Vice President of Operations position and will follow up next week to schedule an appointment."

3. Cover letters must have a theme and clearly communicate who you are, the value you bring to an organization, and your core competencies, qualifications and achievements. Paint a clear picture of who you are; no one will take the time to figure it if you don't spell it out.

4. Stay away from cover letters that just say, "Here's my resume ... give me a job." Be sure your cover letters communicate "WHY" someone should give you the job. The best strategy is, "Here's my resume ... this is why I'm a great candidate ... now, give me a job."

5. Presentation is critical. Your cover letters must be perfect!

Use Your Cover Letters To Highlight

- Significant Career Achievements
- Major Projects & Programs
- Technology Advances
- Large Team & Staff Responsibilities
- International Experience
- Training & Leadership Performance
- Foreign Language Skills
- Capital & Operating Cost Reductions
- Product Development & Launch
- Domestic & International Expansion
- Public Speaking & Publications
- Start-Up & Growth Experience
- Turnaround Management
- Finance and Budget Performance
- Mergers & Acquisitions

- Revenue Gains
- Profit Improvements
- Market Share Ratings
- Productivity Improvements
- Quality Improvements
- Efficiency Improvements
- Computer Proficiency
- Major Contract Negotiations
- Key Account Successes
- Educational Credentials
- Industry Credentials
- Licenses & Registrations
- Teaching Experience
- Joint Ventures & Alliances
- Strategic Partnerships

Highlight only that which is relevant to the type(s) of positions to which you are applying. This above list is provided to give you "food for thought" in identifying, selecting and highlighting the qualifications, competencies and achievements you offer that are most marketable to your specific job search audience.

Types of Cover Letters

You should be prepared to develop six different types of cover letters in order to build your arsenal of dynamic letter communications.

1. **Advertisement Response Cover Letters**
   A. Bullet Format Advertisement Response Cover Letter
   B. Two-Column Advertisement Response Cover Letter
   C. No-Resume Advertisement Response Cover Letter

2. **Targeted Cover Letters for Companies, Recruiters & Venture Capital Firms**
   A. Leadership Cover Letter
   B. Action & Results Cover Letter

3. **Broadcast Letters**

4. **Broadcast Fax Cover Letters**

5. **Network Contact Cover Letters**

6. **Colleague Member Cover Letters**

Let's examine each of these types along with examples illustrating the contents of each cover letter. These examples set the stage for reviewing all examples in the remaining sections of this book.

Ad Response Cover Letters (1A & 1B)

If a company and a recruiter is working to fill a specific position, it is critical to address the specific requirements of that position in your cover letter. Do not make your reader search for the qualifications they require. Rather, spell them out clearly and succinctly for quick review and immediate action.

There are two basic formats for Ad Response Letters - the Bullet Format and the Two-Column Format. Both will communicate your qualifications in direct relation to the specific requirements of the position.

No-Resume Advertisement Response Cover Letter (1C)

There may be occasions when it is appropriate to forward only a cover letter (no resume) in response to an advertisement. This is the best strategy to use when you really are not the "perfect" candidate for a position, but have a unique set of skills, experiences and competencies directly related to the advertised position. To best communicate those competencies, prepare a detailed cover letter that focuses on specific position requirements and how you meet them.

In the following example, the job search candidate had years of university and related teaching/training experience, but had worked as a senior management executive with a sophisticated engineering, technology and product development company for the past 15+ years. His challenge was to highlight his university experience and leadership skills, and not focus on recent career experience. He wanted to position himself as an academic, not a corporate executive. Not only did this letter communicate his value to the university, it got him an interview!

Bullet Format Advertisement Response Cover Letter

DAN R. GREEN
9845 Beverly Glen Street #201
Los Angeles, CA 90087
Phone/Fax: (310) 837-3837 • Email: dml@orb.net.com

August 12, 1996

Barbara Van Alman, HR Director
American Cards
9348 North Pacific Avenue
Los Angeles, CA 93736

Dear Ms. Van Alman:

I am a well-qualified Finance Director writing in response to your advertisement for a Vice President of Finance. Highlights of my professional career include:

- Thirteen years' experience in Corporate and Investment Finance, Treasury, Banking, Financial Reporting, Accounting and Corporate Development.
- Introduction of leading edge MIS and PC applications to automate the entire corporate finance and accounting function.
- Training and development of top-producing finance and accounting professionals.
- Strong analytical, decision making and problem-solving skills.

Recruited to NNC in 1990, I was the driving force behind the development of a sophisticated corporate finance organization. During my six-year tenure, as the company's sales increased 75%, I was able to build the systems, policies and procedures to manage growth with no additional staffing or capital requirements.

NNC has recently brought in a new management team and realigned the workforce. As such, my interest in your search and request for a personal interview. As requested, my compensation requirements are $100,000+ and, of course, I am open to relocation. Thank you.

Sincerely,

Dan R. Green

Enclosure

Two-Column Advertisement Response Cover Letter

BRUCE GRAPESTERN
9712 Outback Way
Lewiston, Idaho 87539

Voice: 815-836-2735   Email: grape@aol.com   Fax: 815-836-3642

January 22, 1997

Roger Maxwell, President & CEO
ABC Companies
900 Southeast B Street
Ontario, CA 93650

Dear Mr. Maxwell:

Not only do I meet your qualifications for Sales Director, I far exceed them.

Your Requirements:	My Qualifications:
Ten Years' Sales & Marketing Experience	Fifteen years' sales & marketing experience in the U.S., Europe, Latin America and the Far East, 12 of which have been at the managerial and director level.
Success In New Product Launch	Creative and strategic leadership of 22 new product launches with combined first year sales of more than $300 million at an average profit margin of 28%.
MBA Degree	MBA Degree from Thunderbird in addition to 100+ hours of continuing executive education.

Having recently resigned my position with IBM, I am now ready for new challenges and new opportunities. Confident that I can deliver results well beyond your expectations, I encourage you to review my resume which clearly communicates my ability to plan, lead and produce. Be advised that my recent salary has averaged $250,000+.

Sincerely,

Bruce Grapestern

Enclosure

SAMUEL G. GLENNSON
160 Igloo Stone Way
Sacramento, CA 94930-3937
Phone/Fax (987) 383-3740 • Messages (987) 715-3768

May 7, 1997

Trevor R. Smith
University of California, San Diego
La Jolla Village Drive
Suite 928
La Jolla, CA 92037

Dear Mr. Smith:

Please accept this letter and enclosed resume as my application for the position of Director of Science, Engineering and Environmental Studies as advertised in the San Diego Union Tribune. I bring to the position a unique blend of qualifications and experience spanning both academic and corporate environments. Highlights include:

- Strong qualifications in Teaching & Academic Administration. During my tenure with Stevens Institute of Technology, I designed and taught graduate and undergraduate courses in Chemistry, Technology and Science. Administrative responsibilities included program development, instructor recruitment, budgeting, resource management, and staff training/supervision. Most significantly, I negotiated and managed cooperative research, R&D and technology projects with corporate partners in the plastics and composites industries.

- More than 20 years experience in Science, Engineering & Environmental Technology. Possess excellent "hands-on" experience in R&D, new product development and new product commercialization in combination with 10+ years of senior-level project and organization management. Technical achievements include 6 U.S. patents and publication of 20 technical papers, 6 course manuals, 2 dissertations, 2 book chapters and 1 textbook.

9

- Development of innovative technical training programs. Throughout my career, I pioneered the development and successful implementation of six graduate training courses and seminars in Polymer Science and Advanced Composites. These programs were subsequently used to train more than 2000 professionals worldwide over the next 10 years at conferences and seminars sponsored by the Society of Plastics Engineers, The Center for Professional Development and several university extension divisions (e.g., UCLA, North Carolina State University, George Washington University).

- Expertise in public/private partnerships. In both my academic and corporate careers, I have functioned as the direct liaison between corporate, industrial, institutional and technical facilities/organizations nationwide to orchestrate cooperative training/technology development programs.

- Success in leading cross-functional teams. I have coordinated research teams of up to 18 professionals from business, government, research and academic institutions. A great deal of our scientific success resulted from my ability to facilitate cooperation among different groups to achieve common project goals and objectives.

- Strong academic qualifications. Ph.D. (Chemistry & Polymer Science), M.Sc. (Chemistry & Biopolymer Science) and B.Sc. (Chemical Engineering).

I have always enjoyed and excelled within an academic environment that fosters innovation and creativity, much like UC - San Diego. To have the opportunity to work with the University would be an ideal career opportunity where I guarantee to provide strong technical and managerial leadership.

Often characterized as the "*Scientist's Business Man*," I bring a bottom-line financial perspective to the discipline of Science and understand the tremendous value to be gained through strategic partnerships and alliances. In turn, I deliver results that are financially measurable and scientifically prominent. I look forward to pursuing this opportunity and thank you in advance for your consideration.

Sincerely,

Samuel G. Glennson

Targeted Cover Letters (2A & 2B)

Targeted cover letters are used to contact companies, recruiters, venture capital firms and any other prospective employer/organization. These are often referred to as "cold call" letters — letters inquiring about employment opportunities and not in response to specific advertisements.

What defines these letters — rather than a specific position — is how you want to position yourself. Do you want to create the vision that your are a Senior Operating Executive? A Senior Sales & Marketing Director? Corporate Finance Executive? Manufacturing Manager? Technology Executive? You must be clear to communicate precisely your message.

In many instances, you can use the same cover letter directed at multiple targets with only minor changes in either the introductory paragraph and/or the closing paragraph. For example:

- When writing to a company, highlight the value you bring to the company.

- When writing to a recruiter, highlight the value you bring to their client company.

- When writing to a venture capital firm, highlight the value you bring to their portfolio companies.

> **To all of your Targeted Cover Letter audiences,**
> **communicate the same message:**
> **Performance, Action & Results!**

The Leadership Letter (2A)

The <u>Leadership Letter</u> is an aggressive tool that effectively communicates your leadership competencies and performance. When a Chairman, CEO, President or other executive makes the decision to hire a new member for his/her executive management team, the single most critical attribute that a prospective candidate must bring to their organization is the ability to lead companies, organizations, divisions, programs, projects, staffs and cross-functional teams. Results and performance are, of course, critical. However, a prospective employer will focus on identifying a candidate who can not only produce, but brings strong, decisive and visionary leadership competencies to their organization.

Action & Results Cover Letter (2B)

The <u>Action & Results Cover Letter</u> provides a strong presentation of the 3-5 most significant achievements of your career, highlighting those achievements that are most related to your current career objectives and/or the specific requirements of an advertised position. Action & Results Letters are bold in demonstrating performance and quantifiable achievements. They clearly communicate the message, "I produce and deliver."

<u>**Use these cover letters to target**</u>:

- **Companies**
- **Recruiters**
- **Venture Capital Firms**

CHRISTOPHER FRANKLIN

259 Court Street
Greenwich, Connecticut 06495
Home: (203) 738-3938   Email: cfrank@msn.com   Office: (202) 378-3755

March 10, 1997

Anthony Arnold, President & CEO
Top Cat Apparel
2888 Island View
Garden City, NY 11542

Dear Mr. Arnold:

High-growth companies require leadership that is broad in perspective, merging all core disciplines to achieve corporate goals and deliver aggressive performance results. In my career, I have done just that. With more than 15 years of senior-level management experience, I personally directed virtually all core operating, strategic, marketing and financial functions. Most significantly, I delivered strong performance in earnings, cost reduction, process improvement and business development.

High-growth companies also require visionary leadership. It is not enough to manage the day-to-day operations. It is critical that the leadership team provide direction and decisive action.

- In my current turnaround position, I am creating and implementing strategic and tactical plans to build revenues by 10%-15% over the next year.
- Previously, as General Manager, I captured $13 million in cost reductions, introduced advanced technology and improved quality ratings to above 97%.
- In my entrepreneurial venture, I transitioned a concept into a fully-operational business, negotiated seed financing and achieved profitability in the first year.

Currently, I am involved in an interim management situation and, as such, am exploring new career challenges. I'll phone next week to schedule an interview at your convenience.

Sincerely,

Christopher Franklin

Action & Results Cover Letter

WENDELL BROWN

9821 Ranchers Way   •   Richardson, Texas 93875   •   (654) 839-2625

June 5, 1997

Carson Dillar, President
LJK Lamont
1986 Fifth Avenue
Denver, CO 30975

Dear Mr. Dillar:

Building corporate value is my expertise — value that is measured in increased revenues, improved earnings, reduced operating costs and more competitive market advantages. It is this expertise, along with strong strategic planning, financial, M&A and operating management skills, that I bring to LJK Lamont. Highlights include:

- Between 1992 and 1997, I led the successful turnaround of Diabolique, Inc., delivering a 250% improvement in net profit and 50%+ gain in annual revenues (40% of which was generated from new products/new markets).

- Between 1988 and 1991, with full P&L responsibility for a Cramer business unit, I reduced costs by $2 million and drove revenue growth of 40% to close the fiscal year at $250 million (with 30% increase in net profitability).

- Between 1982 and 1987, I reengineered two of Gilart's business units, negotiated six successful acquisitions and positioned the company as the #1 metals producer in both U.S. and European markets.

Currently, I am exploring new executive opportunities where I can continue to drive domestic and/or international market growth while providing strong "hands-on" P&L and operating leadership. As such, my interest in meeting with you to evaluate your needs and the long-term vision of LJK Lamont. I'll be in Denver the week of July 1 and look forward to meeting with you then. I'll phone next week to schedule a convenient time. Thank you.

Sincerely,

Wendell Brown

Broadcast Letter (3)

The <u>Broadcast Letter</u> is perhaps the most controversial job search marketing communication because it is used in place of a resume. It is generally one full page (sometimes two) and is written to capture your reader's attention through the innovative presentation of skills, professional competencies and results.

Broadcast letters avoid the pre-programmed behaviors of resume review which can include (1) forwarding it to the Human Resources Department, (2) setting it aside for review as time permits, or (3) depositing it in the "circular file." With a Broadcast Letter, you are delivering a personal piece of correspondence with no visual cues as to the purpose. An individual must read (or at least peruse) the letter to determine its content, allowing you the opportunity to communicate your message. If, after reading your letter, the prospective employer or recruiter is interested in exploring your qualifications, he/she will ask for your resume. In turn, the same resume that may have been thrust aside is now eagerly awaited.

Broadcast Fax Letter (4)

The <u>Broadcast Fax Letter</u> is the "latest and greatest" in technologically-driven job search because it is "immediate." There is great controversy over whether or not to include a resume with a Broadcast Fax Cover Letter. One school of thought believes that the letter itself should be enough to lure a phone call. You've given just enough information to "whet someone's appetite." The other school of thought believes that the resume enclosure is critical in substantiating the achievement(s) in your cover letter and establishing your credibility. My recommendation is the latter. I believe the resume is an invaluable tool in demonstrating the value, worth and strength you bring to an organization. There are computer programs available that automatically fax a cover letter to hundreds of companies or recruiters with the "push of a button," making Broadcast Fax Letters a quick, easy and inexpensive job search tool.

$$\boxed{\textbf{Broadcast Letter}}$$

LORETTA LEWIS
56543 Frau Kapplein
Germany
011-49-455-467-9432
US Voice Mail (312) 999-9987

April 23, 1997

John Q. Public
President & CEO
Lester Aims Smith Recruiters, Inc.
222 Promenade Lane
New York, NY 10020

Dear Mr. Public:

On January 12, 1997, Amelia (my precocious four year old daughter) turned down her peanut butter and jelly sandwich and (Achtung!) chose a liverwurst on rye toast instead — a somewhat un-American act, you might say. I had been thinking about writing to you before, but that solitary act alone clearly communicated the message that it's time the Lewis Family moved back to the US before they irretrievably become German instead of American.

You'll never find me over here (after five years, my trail at home is a little cold), so I'm writing to you instead. Can you get a great consumer services, durables and packaged goods marketing and advertising executive back to the land of baseball, apple pie and Chevrolet? I am currently Executive VP of a worldwide advertising agency whose name you should know. A little background:

- To lead an advertising agency or marketing and sales efforts of a major corporation, excellent leadership skills are essential. Here's an even tougher test: Attract, mold, teach and lead a team of German (and other European) creative and operations personnel (in their own languages) in American-style marketing and promotional strategies. Against entrenched competition. With less money. On shorter creative and client review cycles. You get the idea. Ask me about our successes with Delta Airlines, Wella, Grand Met, Unilever and others.

- Successful marketing campaigns aren't always offensive — sometimes the best solution is an ironclad defense. For a large German-based consumer packaged goods company, we stopped Father Procter dead in his tracks (then mugged him and picked his pockets). I would be pleased to tell you about my role in making the German company P&G's chief nemesis in Europe. By my calculations, P&G's massive advertising and marketing investment went down the drain.

- There is much, much more to tell. Thirteen solid years in advertising with Fortune 500 companies (made Wella a European household name; helped convert McDonald's breakfast hockey pucks to sausage and egg biscuits). My language affinity is unusual for an American; I'm fluent in six languages (eight if I could email Socrates and Julius Caesar). Two degrees from Harvard and an MBA from The University of Chicago.

To find out more about me and what I might do for your consumer packaged goods/services/durables client, please call me and let's talk. I check my Chicago voice mail regularly or you can call me in Germany (but please don't wake up the Lewis Family at 3 a.m. — Central European time is EST plus six hours).

Sincerely,

Loretta Lewis

GRETA GREEN
122 Smith Road
Wormont, NH 02303
(603) 777-9867

May 12, 1997

Greg Amandro
The Amandro Agency
122 Park Avenue
New York, NY 10022

Dear Mr. Amandro:

Are you interested in an executive who generated $100 million in sales over two years for a Fortune 100 consumer products company?

Call me.

Sincerely,

Greta Green

Enclosure

Network Contact Cover Letter (5)

The <u>Network Contact Cover Letter</u> is the ideal marketing communication to forward to your network of professional contacts, colleagues, associates and acquaintances. We know how vital your network contacts are to your job search. Produce a winning cover letter that is sharp, upscale and achievement-driven. Your goal is to entice your contacts to "go to work for you" by helping you expand your contacts, open doors to prospective employers and facilitate your accelerated job search.

Colleague Member Cover Letter (6)

The <u>Colleague Member Cover Letter</u> is the ideal marketing tool to communicate with members of professional associations of which you are a member. Leverage your common affiliation to your advantage and tap into the professional network of contacts of other members. You will be amazed as how positive the results are and delighted with the subsequent opportunities that may present themselves.

COVER LETTER DYNAMICS

INTRODUCTION: Capture your reader's attention with a clear statement of your expertise.

CONTENT: Highlight your skills, competencies, achievements and success most related to a specific position, employer, industry or profession.

CLOSING: Ask for the interview!

Network Contact Cover Letter

ANDREW W. BELLINGER III
188 Roest Road
White Plains, New York 12037
Home Phone (212) 333-3333   Voice Mail (875) 382-3720

June 1, 1997

John Holter
XYZ Technology Venture
111 East Main Street
Minneapolis, MN 37483

Dear John:

It has been a long time! In fact, I believe that the last time we spoke was about two years ago at IBM's annual sales leadership convention, just before you left to join 3M. So much has transpired since then that I wanted to update you. After all these years, I've decided to leave IBM and pursue new sales management opportunities.

Most significantly, I was promoted last year to National Sales Manager for Emerging Technologies. Over the past year, I've recruited a team of seven Account Managers, established a coast-to-coast distribution network, and closed $25 million in contracts. Our success has been phenomenal and IBM is projecting a 200% gain in revenues in 18 months.

I'm sure you're wondering why I'm considering a change at this point and with such a successful venture just launched. Jenny and I have decided that we want to return to the Midwest and to a more relaxed life-style. After all these years in New York City, we've had enough!

If you know of an organization in need of strong and decisive sales leadership, I would welcome a referral or contact name. The best way to reach me is on my voice mail at (875) 382-3720. My best to Linda and your kids. Thanks for your help.

Yours truly,

Andrew W. Bellinger III

MARTIN D. DERMOD
736 Read Street
Spokane, Washington 93775
Home (777) 393-9372   Fax (777) 393-9373

May 17, 1997

Lester Legume, Executive Vice President
Energy Venture Technology Company
372 Orange Avenue
Atlanta, GA 30093

Dear Lester:

A member of the American Marketing Association since 1989, I've gained invaluable knowledge and insight into our industry. Through networking and direct communication with colleagues nationwide, I've expanded my skill set, sharpened my product knowledge and elevated my professional status. I'm sure your experience with AMA has been just as valuable to your career.

One of my greatest contributions to the membership has been my role on the Training & Development Committee. In fact, not only have I participated in the design of new educational programs, I also guided many of these individuals through successful job search campaigns. Now, I'm looking to the membership, and to you in particular, for such assistance.

A 19-year veteran of Johnson & Johnson, I've progressed from early field sales positions to my current assignment as Director of Marketing for our #1 product line. In this capacity, my team and I delivered 49% growth in U.S. markets and 67% growth in Europe/Asia.

Currently, I am exploring new professional opportunities in a senior-level marketing leadership assignment. I prefer to remain in the Western U.S., but would, of course, look at opportunities elsewhere. If you are aware of an organization in need of strong and decisive marketing leadership, I would certainly appreciate the referral and a contact name. Thanks for your assistance.

Sincerely,

Martin D. Dermod

Enclosure

Two Other Critical Cover Letters to Accelerate Your Job Search

Sponsor Cover Letters

Have a great senior-level contact who thinks highly of your experience and performance? An individual who will attest to the quality and strength of your career track? Have this individual write a personal letter to his/her network of contacts notifying them of your availability and highlighting the value you bring to their organization.

Refer to the Section entitled **"Sponsor Letters"** to review several samples. See pages 247-249.

Interview Follow-Up Letter - Mandatory or Optional?

Interview Follow-Up Letters are mandatory in today's job search market. Not only are they considered proper etiquette, these letters allow you to communicate important messages and vital information to the hiring organization.

Once you've had the opportunity to interview with a company, you will be aware of their key issues and goals. Are they focused on increasing revenues? Reducing costs? Improving organizational efficiency? Expanding internationally? Resolving production problems? The list is endless.

Use your Interview Follow-Up Letter to communicate how you can solve their problems, improve their operations, generate profits and meet their goals. This letter is the ideal forum to directly respond to the employer's needs and clearly state your ability to deliver results. With this letter you create a sense of immediate action.

Interview Follow-Up Letters can vary widely in length, from one page to numerous pages, depending upon the messages you want to communicate and the depth of information you wish to provide. Often these letters are prepared in direct response to questions proposed either by a company or a recruiter. In this instance, length is not a consideration. Focus your efforts on substantial text and results.

Refer to the Section entitled **"Interview Follow-Up Letters"** to review several samples. See pages 250-264.

Frequently Asked Cover Letter Questions

1. **You are a top-flight candidate with precisely the qualifications and experience Must cover letters be one page?**

   Generally, but not always. Keep your cover letters to one page in most instances. However, there will be occasions where more than one page is appropriate in order to effectively communicate your message.

2. **What is the difference between a cover letter and a broadcast letter?**

   A cover letter is a marketing communication that accompanies your resume. A broadcast letter is a marketing communication that is forwarded instead of your resume. Refer to the previous section on Broadcast Letters to determine the appropriate instances for using this type of marketing communication instead of the more "traditional" cover letter with accompanying resume.

3. **If writing "cold" to a company (not in response to a specific advertisement), should I send my resume and cover letter to the Human Resources Department?**

NO! HR Departments "process" and evaluate resumes. They generally do not make hiring decisions. Instead, send your resume to the President, CEO, COO, Vice President of Sales & Marketing, or another senior executive with the authority to schedule an interview and make a hiring decision. It is much more efficient to work "down from the top" than to start with the HR Department.

4. **Must I respond to salary information if requested in an advertisement, by a recruiter or by a company?**

YES! If the information is requested, it is recommended that you respond. It is not necessary at this point to include a detailed salary review of your entire career. Rather, you might write, "As requested, my recent salary has averaged $95,000 to $115,000."

If a company requests salary requirements, you do not have to list a specific number. Rather, "My salary requirements are $150,000+, but flexible based upon the requirements and demands of the position."

In either instance, your goal is to only "define the ballpark" at this point in the hiring process. Further discussions regarding compensation will follow through the various phases of the interview process.

5. **Should my cover letter be on the same paper as my resume?**

YES - generally. You want to deliver a sharp, professional presentation. If the documents do not match, be sure they are complementary. For example, if you have prepared your resume on a light gray paper with a white border, prepare your cover letters on matching white paper. The presentation is upscale and distinctive.

6. **Should I mail my resumes and cover letters in large envelopes (9"x12")
   or   regular #10 envelopes?**

I have listened to 45-minute discussions about envelope size. Have YOU ever
made a hiring decision based on size of envelope? Probably not.

Use #10 envelopes for most of your mailings. Use the larger envelopes for
high-level network contacts, direct mail to senor executives and high-end
advertisements. It makes sense. If sending your resume to Bill Gates, don't
fold it into a little envelope. However, if mailing resumes to 500 recruiters, the
small envelopes are fine and less expensive. Use your judgement and follow
your instincts.

7. **Should I use monarch size paper for my cover letters?**

Monarch paper does stand out from the more traditional letter size paper and
appears more personal. However, in my career in executive job search and
career marketing, I have never found that size of paper made any difference in
determining whether or not an individual is going to extend you the opportunity
for an interview. I leave monarch size paper to your discretion.

8. **If I've faxed or emailed a cover letter and resume to a prospective employer or recruiter, how should I follow up?**

ALWAYS follow up with a hard copy in the mail. This accomplishes two things:
(1) gets your name and credentials in front of them again, and (2) provides a
more upscale, more dynamic and more visually pleasing presentation than the
fax or email copy.

9. Should I follow up with phone calls after I've sent a letter and resume?

Telephone follow up can be quite costly and it is often difficult to get the person you wish to speak to on the phone. Try calling at off-hours and be persistent. Also, be sure to position yourself well with the secretary or assistant of the individual you are attempting to contact. The secretary/assistant can be your single most valuable asset in opening the door and getting you in.

However, I do not recommend telephone follow up after each and every letter and resume you forward unless you have a contact at the company, consider yourself an ideal candidate, or are particularly interested in that company or position. It is a better use of your time to get more resumes and cover letters out than spending your days leaving phone messages.

10. How do I address a cover letter if I do not have a contact name?

"Dear Sir/Madam" is the most acceptable salutation. However, if possible, make a telephone call to the company and get a contact name. It is certainly much better to write to someone specifically, rather than to anyone. Further, you then have a contact name for future follow up.

Salary History & Salary Requirements

What Is A Salary History?

A Salary History is a listing of your past positions with beginning and ending salaries. The Salary History, if truly comprehensive, will include not only your salary, but your bonuses, incentives and other compensation.

What Are Salary Requirements?

Your Salary Requirements are your current salary objective, and can be (1) presented as a specific number ("My salary requirement is $100,000 annually plus complete benefits package", or (2) as a range ("My salary requirements are $100,000 to $135,000 annually.")

If you are unable to provide your salary requirements, at least indicate that "My salary requirements are flexible depending upon the scope and responsibility of the position."

When Do You Include Salary In Your Cover Letter?

1. When asked for in an advertisement.

2. When writing to recruiters.

And, generally, not at any other time. Salary is not a topic to be discussed in a cover letter unless specifically asked for and/or expected. It is a much better strategy to discuss salary history and requirements in a person-to-person interview where you can ask questions regarding salary ranges, past compensation of previous individuals in the position for which you are applying and competitive market/industry compensation.

Salary is often a very difficult topic to discuss in a cover letter — particularly if you know little about a specific position or a specific company. You don't want to state a figure that is too high and will put you "out of the running." However, you don't want to "low ball" your worth either.

Cover Letter KeyWords & Action Verbs

Use these nouns and verbs to communicate your skills, competencies and track record of performance.

Acquisitions

Benchmarking

Best in Class

Catalyst

Change Agent

Competitive Market Positioning

Cross-Cultural Communications

Cross-Functional Team Leadership

Electronic Commerce

Emerging Growth Venture

Entrepreneurial Drive

Entrepreneurial Vision

High-Growth

High-Impact

High-Performance

Internet Technology

Joint Ventures

Market Revitalization

Mergers

Multinational Organization

New Media

Organizational Development

Organizational Leader

Outsourcing

Partnerships

Performance Improvement

Performance Reengineering

Process Redesign & Improvement

Productivity & Efficiency Improvement

Quality Assurance

Strategic Alliances

Team Building

Total Quality Management

High-Impact Cover Letter Phrases

Use these phrases to aggressively communicate the strength of your qualifications, performance and results.

Accelerating Revenue Growth

Aggressive Turnaround Leadership

Capturing Cost Reductions

Competitively Positioning Products & Technologies

Cross-Culturally Sensitive

Delivering Strong & Sustainable Revenue Gains

Distinguished Performance

Driving Product Development & Innovation

Fast-Track Promotion

Matrix Management

Outperforming Global Competition

Pioneering Technologies

Start-Up, Turnaround & High-Growth Organizations

Strong & Sustainable Financial Gains

Strong & Sustainable Performance Gains

Technologically-Sophisticated Organizations

Visionary Leadership

Personality Descriptors for Cover Letters

Use these words to communicate "who you are" with a focus on both personal and professional attributes.

Aggressive	Entrepreneurial
Analytical	Independent
Competitive	Persuasive
Courageous	Positive
Creative	Pragmatic
Customer-Driven	Resourceful
Decisive	Sophisticated
Diligent	Strong
Diplomatic	Successful
Dynamic	Talented

LOOK FOR:

"1500+ Keywords for $100,000+ Jobs:
Tools for Building Powerful, Winning Resumes"

A comprehensive compilation of KeyWords, Action Verbs, High-Impact Phrases and Personality Descriptors for creating powerful resumes, cover letters and job search marketing communications.
Due in bookstores in February 1998.

CHAPTER 2

COVER LETTER SAMPLES

Following are 201 cover letter samples, categorized by job function/profession and written specifically for management, senior management and executive job search candidates. Use these cover letters to get ideas, concepts, strategies, structures, formats and words to develop your own cover letters — for advertisement responses, targeted direct mail, recruiters, venture capital firms, "cold calls" and network/professional contacts.

Look carefully at each sample. There is a specific strategy for how and why every cover letter was prepared — a strategy based on each individual's career track, achievements and objectives. Choose the best from each that is appropriate to your career, accomplishments, competencies and goals.

Feel free to duplicate specific content, phrases, formats and styles. That's why you bought this book!

ACCOUNTING & AUDIT

KeyWords, Action Verbs & High-Impact Phrases

To "Nail" Your Cover Letter:

*   General Accounting & Cost Accounting

*   Accounting Information Systems Technology

*   Cost Reductions & Avoidance

*   Financial Planning, Analysis & Reporting

*   Internal & External Audit Management

*   Budgeting, Forecasting & Projections

*   Process Design & Efficiency Improvement

*   Integrated Accounting Systems & Consolidation

*   Banking & Cash Flow Management

*   Credit & Collections Management

STUART GRANT, CPA, CMA
21547 South Washington Avenue
Morristown, New Jersey 08654

Home (908) 491-5471

Office (201) 655-5410 x110

May 16, 1997

Ronald Keeler
President
Pacific Manufacturing, Inc.
1234 Grant Highway, Suite 5472
Los Angeles, CA 90054

Dear Mr. Keeler:

Recruited to LLC Industries in 1984, I spearheaded the development and management of all corporate accounting operations for over 12 years as the company grew, expanded, acquired, merged and reconfigured itself several times. The challenges were enormous and the opportunity tremendous.

My role with the corporation expanded beyond corporate accounting to include active participation with the executive and operating management teams in strategic planning and corporate development. Involved in numerous mergers, acquisitions and divestitures, I not only provided the "numbers" but also the rationale, strategy and action plans to achieve our results.

As you review my resume, you will note that I have extensive qualifications in all corporate accounting and financial reporting functions in combination with extensive skills in debt management/restructuring, cash management and related corporate treasury functions. I am a decisive business manager with excellent planning and problem solving skills, eager to take on new challenges and deliver results.

Currently, I am exploring new professional opportunities and would welcome a personal interview for the position of Corporate Accounting Director as advertised in the Search Bulletin. I appreciate your time and consideration, and look forward to meeting with you.

Sincerely,

Stuart Grant, CPA, CMA

Enclosure

DOLORES M. LOREAN
9845 Beverley Glen Street #102
Los Angeles, California 90087
(310) 977-6544

August 12, 1997

Barbara Van Sprecken
Director of Human Resources
American Greeting Cards
9348 North Pacific Avenue
Los Angeles, CA 97764

Dear Ms. Van Sprecken:

I am a well-qualified Accounting Professional/Accounting Supervisor writing in response to your advertisement for a Manager of Accounting. Highlights of my professional career include:

* Thirteen years' experience in Accounts Receivable, Billing, Credit/Collection, Accounts Payable and Accounting/Financial Reporting.

* Introduction of leading edge MIS and PC applications to automate manual accounting functions, increase data accuracy and reduce monthly closing cycles.

* Training and development of accounting professionals and support staff.

* Extensive qualifications in customer relationship management, communications and negotiations.

* Excellent analytical, decision making and problem-solving skills.

Recruited to Investment News in 1990, I was the driving force behind the development of a sophisticated accounts receivable system. During my five-year tenure, as the company sales increased 75%, I was able to build the systems, policies, procedures and standards to manage growth with no additional staff. Our results were significant and measurable.

Investment News has recently brought in a new management team and realigned the workforce. Thus my interest in your search and request for a personal interview. Thank you.

Sincerely,

Dolores M. Lorean

Enclosure

JENNIFER A. MARIETTA
5274 Roundabout Drive
Athens, Georgia 33858

Home (770) 414-6470

Office (770) 515-6547

February 27, 1997

W.R. Grace & Company
c/o Dept. TF
1 Town Center Road
Boca Raton, FL 33486-1010

Dear Sir/Madam:

In need of a **Director of Internal Audit**? Let me tell you why I'm the perfect candidate:

- Eight years of progressively responsible experience in the design, development and leadership of large-scale internal audit organizations (financial, IS and operational).

- Success in transitioning audit from an internal "regulatory" function into a cooperative business partner to all operating units, responsive to their constantly changing operating, market and financial demands.

- Extensive IS experience throughout my career with recent leadership responsibility (in cooperation with other management executives) for a multi-million dollar SAP implementation.

- Record of fast-track career promotion, based on combined strength of management, leadership, analytical, technology and project management skills. Current responsibility for financial affairs of 50 business units nationwide.

- Consistent and verifiable contributions to improved revenues and profits through process redesign, internal controls, cost reduction and performance improvement initiatives.

Although secure in my current position, I am confidentially exploring new professional challenges and opportunities. Thus my interest in interviewing for the position of Director of Internal Audit where I guarantee to provide strong, decisive and results-driven leadership.

I appreciate your time in reviewing my qualifications and look forward to speaking with you.

Sincerely,

Jennifer A. Marietta

Enclosure

35

ADMINISTRATION

KeyWords, Action Verbs & High-Impact Phrases

To "Nail" Your Cover Letter:

* Project Management

* Record Keeping & Administration

* VIP & Board Relations

* Correspondence Management

* Office Administration & Management

* Executive Liaison Affairs

* Productivity & Efficiency Improvement

* Telecommunications Systems Management

* Vendor & Supplier Relations

* Employee Relations & Communications

PETER C. ROSS
1505 Cherry Tree Lane
Frederick, Maryland 25471
(410) 259-5419

March 16, 1997

President
KRT Ventures
3987 Arlington Circle
Washington, D.C. 20054

Dear Sir/Madam:

As Director of Administration for three successful businesses in the past 12 years, I have introduced the systems, processes and methods to increase productivity, improve efficiency and expand service capabilities. By integrating the capabilities of a well-trained staff with sophisticated PC technology, I have delivered strong operating results.

The demands of each organization have been challenging and required tremendous effort in creating appropriate business management and administrative functions. My ability to build cooperative working relationships with both professional and support staff has been a key factor in meeting our goals and achieving our success.

Key areas of focus throughout my career have included human resources, purchasing, contracts, facilities, information technology, strategic planning and customer service. In addition, I have spearheaded a number of marketing, advertising and business development projects that have contributed to growth and improved profitability.

Although secure in my current position, I have decided to pursue new opportunities. As such, my interest in KRT Ventures and request for a personal interview. Thank you.

Sincerely,

Peter C. Ross

Enclosure

FRANK M. EDWARDS

4958 King Street
Rockville Centre, New York 10567

Home (516) 554-5471
Office (212) 654-7644

August 25, 1997

Box T938
The New York Times
New York, NY 10801

Dear Sir/Madam:

I am writing in response to your advertisement for a Technology Director and have enclosed my resume for your review. Highlights of my professional career that may be of particular interest to you include:

- Team leadership of a $100 million project to create the most comprehensive and most technologically-sophisticated library in the U.S. Efforts involved project planning, staffing, technology installation and all financial affairs.

- Participation in the acquisition/implementation of the largest-ever smart card technology to control billing for 500+ computers.

- Design and implementation of work processes, efficiencies and productivity improvement initiatives.

- Seven years of experience managing budgeting, accounting, financial reporting, financial analysis, project finance and internal financial controls.

I bring to the position excellent planning, organizational, analytical, training and supervisory skills. Further, I have extensive qualifications in coordinating the efforts of cross-functional project team members.

Although secure in my current position, I am confidentially exploring new professional challenges and opportunities, and would welcome a personal interview for the advertised position. Thank you.

Sincerely,

Frank M. Edwards

Enclosure

MARSHA L. SMITH

2233 Turning Leaf Lane
Chevy Chase, Maryland 20657
(301) 647-4657

July 29, 1997

Robert C. Malcolm
President
Automated Billing, Inc.
3495 Howard Street
Baltimore, MD 20874

Dear Mr. Malcolm:

Throughout my 14-year professional career, I have held diverse management responsibility for the planning, staffing, operations and P&L performance of large-scale administrative organizations (e.g., order entry, billing, customer service, accounts receivable, collections). I have consistently delivered strong operating, productivity, cost and quality gains through workforce reengineering, streamlining operations and quality/performance improvement initiatives. Significant projects and achievements include:

- Led a $115 million customer service/billing organization supporting both commercial and government accounts. Reduced DSO from 100 to 32 days and facilitated the implementation of scanning technology to expedite communications.

- Conducted extensive analyses of nationwide business operations in an aggressive effort to identify strengths/weaknesses, streamline operations and improve overall quality and performance.

- Created a Competency Management System to identify the cross-functional skill/knowledge level for more than 22,000 employees at operating sites throughout the U.S.

These achievements are indicative of the quality and caliber of my entire career — identify the problem, design tools/programs to facilitate change, and drive forward successful implementation. I am direct and decisive, yet flexible in responding to the constantly changing needs of the customer base, my staff and senior management.

Although secure in my current position, I am anxious to transition into a high-growth venture where I can continue to lead top-flight administrative/customer service operations. As such, I would welcome a personal interview to explore opportunities with your organization. Thank you.

Sincerely,

Marsha L. Smith

Enclosure

ADVERTISING & PUBLIC RELATIONS

KeyWords, Action Verbs & High-Impact Phrases

To "Nail" Your Cover Letter:

* Advertising Agency Relations

* Major Campaigns & Client Projects

* Internet & New Media Campaigns

* VIP Relations

* Press Relations & Coverage

* Corporate Communications

* Revenue & Profit Increases

* Special Events Management

* Crisis Communications

* Employee Communications

NANCY FRIEDMAN

1511 Park Avenue, #409
New York, New York 10010
(212) 917-0045

March 31, 1997

Diane M. Woodson
Public Relations Inc.
9834 Commercial Drive, Suite 398
McLean, VA 20354

Dear Ms. Woodson:

Gaining positive public relations and publicity is an art that requires the ability to merge strategy with concept and action. It demands an individual who not only understands the product and the market, but knows the "PR game" and its significant players.

This is the expertise I bring to your organization. With 16 years of top-level public relations, publicity, advertising, marketing and special events experience, I have created winning campaigns that have received positive press coverage and facilitated strong market gains. Most notably, I have demonstrated my flexibility in transitioning PR programs from one industry to another, capitalizing upon the core competencies of each campaign while reinventing tactics to meet specific market demands.

I have often found myself challenged, working in a boardroom of "old line" companies unaware of the tremendous demands and influence of public relations. Being able to communicate the value of PR to these individuals has not only required strong and decisive presentation skills, but the ability to educate regarding the value of sophisticated creativity.

My career has spanned the entire spectrum of the PR market — from Wall Street investors to individual consumers — from leading broadcast media to large employee groups — from individual corporate sponsors to worldwide advertising agencies. To each, I have provided the strategic, tactical and operating leadership critical to communicating our messages and accelerating our growth.

At this juncture in my career, I am seeking a position that will allow me to the opportunity to continue spearheading successful, visible and results-driven publicity and PR campaigns. Thus my interest in your search for a Public Relations Director and request for a personal interview. Thank you.

Sincerely,

Nancy Friedman

Enclosure

MARY R. GLEN
1511 McLean Avenue
Charleston, West Virginia 55413
(304) 917-0045

June 26, 1997

M. Marriot
Coplthorne & Bellows
1021 Crown Point Parkway #340
Atlanta, GA 30338

Dear M. Marriot:

The world of public relations has changed! No longer is PR a "behind the scenes" function churning out press releases. Today, PR is one of the most critical and most visible functions within an successful corporation. A qualified candidate must be strategist, writer, public speaker and more.

This is the expertise I bring to Coplthorne & Bellows. With 16 years professional experience with both PR agencies and direct with companies in the high-tech industry, I have demonstrated my ability to build market recognition, increase customer awareness, and provide the foundation for strong and sustainable revenue growth.

The breadth of my experience spans markets worldwide and includes the complete portfolio of PR functions (e.g., publicity, press relations, print and broadcast communications, multimedia advertising, strategy, special events). I am successful in combining creative talents with more structured general business skills to deliver campaigns that are cost-effective, market-appropriate and profitable. Equally solid is my performance in strategic planning, team building/leadership, organization development, project planning/management and general administrative affairs.

I would welcome the opportunity to interview for your Public Relations Search and can guarantee that the strength of my qualifications will add measurable value to both your operations and your clients. Thank you. I look forward to speaking with you.

Sincerely,

Mary R. Glen

Enclosure

RACHEL S. THOMPSON
565 Lakeside Drive
Spring Mountain, Minnesota 65471
(811) 234-0090

November 4, 1997

Matthew Atkinson
Dunn Corporation
525 University Avenue, Suite 1500
Menlo Park, CA 94025

Dear Mr. Atkinson:

Consider this. In 1996, millions of PR dollars were invested in the promotion of both emerging and well-established information, telecommunications, Internet and multimedia technology companies. Projections for 1997 and 1998 are even stronger, yet the number of PR firms offering such services is still quite limited. In fact, many of the technology companies that are headquartered in the Washington metro area are going to Philadelphia, New York and other major cities for high-quality, high-caliber PR representation.

There is where I can be of value to Dunn Corporation. With 16 years of top-flight PR and account management experience, I have provided both the strategy and the tactical implementation plans to leaders in the technology industry — Apple Computers, Novell, Cericor Technologies, Hewlett Packard, MCI and Landmark Systems Corporation. The scope of my responsibility has ranged from the conceptual design and implementation of PR campaigns for worldwide product launch to issues arising from complex and rapidly-changing regulatory requirements. Further, my success has included both the development of new client relationships as well as the growth, expansion and retention of existing accounts.

Working either as the Principal of my own PR agency or as the full-time Director of Public Relations, I have been the driving force behind numerous successful PR, advertising and marketing initiatives for these organizations. In an agency setting, I have combined creative talents with more structured general business skills to deliver campaigns that are cost-effective, market-appropriate and profitable. In turn, I have created the market and established the image that has driven millions and millions of dollars in new revenues. Equally solid is my performance in strategic planning, P&L management, team building/leadership, organization development, project planning/management and general administrative affairs.

Now my goal is to launch a start-up PR function targeted exclusively to the technology industry, and I am contacting you to explore your potential interest in this and related market opportunities. I would welcome the chance to speak with you to evaluate your interest, share my ideas and determine the potential viability of such an endeavor. I'll follow-up next week to discuss your preliminary interest and how we proceed from this point forward.

Sincerely,

Rachel S. Thompson

Enclosure

BRYAN ALEXANDER

9834 South Atlantic Avenue - Garden City, NY 11550 - (516) 538-5261

November 13, 1997

Metropolitan Public Relations
Attn: Angela
934 Avenue of the Americas, 23rd Floor
New York, NY 10110

FAX (212) 138-6541

Dear Angela:

I am forwarding my resume in response to your advertisement for a Public Relations Professional. Highlights of my professional career that may be of particular interest to you include the following:

- More than 10 years' experience in both Broadcast and Print Journalism.

- Strong background in marketing, public relations, customer relations and copyrighting/editing.

- Extensive network of contacts throughout the New York metro medical community developed through in-depth reporting and feature stories on the healthcare industry.

- Excellent research, data collection, data synthesis and documentation skills.

- Ability to independently plan, prioritize and manage special projects.

- Outstanding skills and competencies in editorial content development.

My goal is to transition my experience into a high-profile marketing/public relations position where I can continue to drive forward growth and corporate recognition. You will find that the combination of my research, writing and reporting qualifications will make a positive and long-lasting impact upon the success of Metropolitan.

I appreciate your time and consideration, and look forward to meeting with you. Thank you.

Sincerely,

Bryan Alexander

Enclosure

TARA GALESFORD

6547 Winding Road
South New Haven, Connecticut 06354

Home   (860) 262-5414
Office   (860) 868-7836

December 1, 1997

Michael Simon
Managing Partner
Riverside Place Advertising
9485 Riverside Place
Newbury, MA 05471

Dear Mr. Simon:

I am currently exploring new professional opportunities. My goal is to transition into an advertising/public relations position where I can utilize my qualifications in:

- Graphics Design & Presentation
- Customer Relationship Management
- Marketing & New Business Development
- Special Events Planning & Management
- Communications & Public Presentations

As you review my resume, you will note that my career has been focused in the areas of administration, project coordination and financial analysis/reporting. Although quite successful in each of these areas, my interests lie in the marketing and business development side of an organization. However, the skills I have acquired in budgeting, project finance, reporting and analysis, will be of significant value in any operation.

I would welcome the opportunity to meet with you to explore opportunities with Riverside Place Advertising and thank you in advance for your consideration.

Sincerely,

Tara Galesford

Enclosure

ASSOCIATION MANAGEMENT

KeyWords, Action Verbs & High-Impact Phrases

To "Nail" Your Cover Letter:

* Board & Foundations Relations

* Staff Training & Leadership

* Operating Cost Reductions

* Member Services Development & Delivery

* Revenue Success

* Legislative & Regulatory Affairs

* Public & Private Partnerships

* Capital Giving & Fundraising

* Member Communications

* Press Affairs, Public Affairs & Public Relations

LESTER W. WATSON
9834 Chicago Avenue
Highland Park, Illinois 60547
(847) 547-6471

July 20, 1997

James P. Carter
Chairman
International Peanut Council
9485 Peanut Lane
Atlanta, Georgia 64721

Dear Mr. Carter:

With 20 years' experience in Association Management, I bring to the International Peanut Council strong management experience and a record of significant financial results. Directing associations with both corporate and individual members, I have consistently delivered strong performance in:

- Revenue & Profit Improvement
- New Member Development & Member Retention
- New Product & New Service Development
- Budgeting, Fundraising & Corporate Giving
- Administrative Management & Organizational Change/Reengineering

As President & CEO, the scope of my responsibility has spanned all association operations — from strategic planning, Board affairs and budgeting/financial management to member services, public relations and corporate liaison affairs. I combine strong leadership and communications skills with the ability to energize teams and initiate action. In turn, financial, service and operating results have improved year after year.

My goal is to secure a new executive position with an association in need of strong and decisive leadership. I guarantee to increase your membership, expand your services and improve your financial results.

I appreciate your time in reviewing my qualifications and look forward to speaking with you.

Sincerely,

Lester W. Watson

Enclosure

DAVID C. TAYLOR
100 Freemont Avenue
Centerport, VA 25794
(540) 564-7647

April 1, 1997

Elizabeth M. Lynch
Executive Director
National Industries For The Blind
3984 H Street
Washington, D.C. 20001

Dear Ms. Lynch:

With more than 15 years of senior-level financial and accounting experience, I have strong competencies in virtually all facets of organizational finance — from general accounting, budgeting and reporting to high-level strategic planning, investment management and PC technology programs. My focus has always been on modernizing existing operations, introducing new systems and competencies, and contributing to improved financial returns.

Having had the opportunity to work within both public and private sector organizations has given me broad-based exposure to the unique components of both for-profit and nonprofit enterprises. This, in turn, has allowed me to deploy the best of both, transferring for-profit strategies into the nonprofit arena to drive financial growth.

Inherent in my responsibilities has been direct leadership of project accounting and finance, funds and grant management, contracting, personnel training, systems development and administration. I am direct and decisive in my leadership style, able to quickly ascertain the root cause of a problem and initiate appropriate corrective action. I enjoy a fast paced and proactive business environment.

My goal at this point in my career is to transition my expertise into the nonprofit arena, and would welcome the opportunity for a personal interview for the position of Finance Director. As requested, my salary history has averaged $75,000 to $115,000 over the past four years.

Thank you.

Sincerely,

David C. Taylor

Enclosure

48

BANKING

KeyWords, Action Verbs & High-Impact Phrases

To "Nail" Your Cover Letter:

* Revenue & Profit Increases

* Operating Cost Reductions

* New Services & New Products

* Technology Installations

* New Sources of Fee Income

* Asset & Portfolio Development & Management

* Bad Debt Recovery & Workout

* Large / High-Profile Financial Transactions

* Reorganization & Consolidation

* Regulatory Performance

DANIEL RICHARDSON
5473 Fourth Avenue
Cleveland, Ohio 45145
(216) 647-6541

February 7, 1997

Paul Buchman
Managing Partner
Buchman Executive Recruiters, Inc.
9834 Wabash Avenue, Suite 394
Chicago, IL 60066

Dear Mr. Buchman:

Building value is my expertise — value that is measured in terms of increased assets, fee income, volume and profit. Whether challenged to lead a start-up, turnaround or high-growth lending and banking organization, I have consistently delivered financial results well beyond projections:

* In my current position as Senior Vice President with Banc One, I orchestrated a successful turnaround and return to profitability while simultaneously managing an aggressive M&A program.
* During my tenure with Eastern Mortgage Corporation, I built the New England region from virtual start-up into a 6-branch, 92-employee business unit with loan production exceeding $350 million annually.
* Subsequently as Senior Vice President with Eastern, I built production to over $1 billion and delivered $17 million in net fee income.

These achievements are indicative of the quality and caliber of my entire professional career — identify and capitalize upon opportunities to win market share, expand customer base and outperform competition. In turn, we have delivered operating achievements well beyond projections, revolutionized our service performance, and captured strong and sustainable financial gains.

Complementing my financial contributions are strong general management qualifications, with particular emphasis in long-range strategic planning, product/service development, human resources, team building and MIS technologies. Further, I have a wealth of experience in loan underwriting, loan processing and quality control, each of which has been critical to the integrity and value of our asset portfolio.

My career with Banc One has been excellent. As my resume indicates, we have transitioned the institution into one of the industry's top-performers. However, due to the nature of the ownership (family), the opportunities for career advancement and continued challenge are minimal. Thus my interest in <u>confidentially</u> pursuing new career alternatives.

If you are working with a client organization in need of strong, decisive and action-driven results, I would welcome a personal interview. Be assured that the depth of my industry experience, unique and effective leadership style, and commitment to improved financial results, will add measurable value to your client. Thank you.

Sincerely,

Daniel Richardson

Enclosure

FELICIA C. URENDA
6547 Collins Avenue
Coral Gables, Florida 31183
(954) 386-7991

January 2, 1997

John Rockwell
President
Florida National Bank
9485 Sunshine Corporate Center, Suite 3934
Miami, Florida 32654

Dear Mr. Rockwell:

I am looking for a great opportunity. With 12 years of increasingly responsible experience in retail and commercial banking operations, I bring to your organization excellent qualifications in:

- Introducing customer service driven initiatives to enhance customer retention, improve customer loyalty and promote new business development.

- Developing and implementing improved business processes to streamline operations, reduce overhead costs and improve overall performance.

- Launching sales and marketing initiatives that have won dominant positioning despite extensive market competition.

Promoted rapidly throughout my career, I advanced to Branch Vice President with the Bank of Miami. My challenge was to enhance the performance of both domestic and international banking operations. Results were impressive and included the negotiation/closure of numerous commercial banking agreements and recognition as a top revenue producer for two consecutive years. Please also note that I have strong qualifications in consumer lending, and am currently managing a high-profile loan marketing and lending operation for Savings of America.

My goal is to join one of the nation's leading banking institutions offering opportunities in the Miami marketplace for long-term employment and career advancement. In turn, I guarantee strong performance, consistently superior results and a real commitment to your organization.

Sincerely,

Felicia C. Urenda

Enclosure

SAMUEL P. ROBINSON
39 East 54th Street, #230
New York, New York 10110
(212) 536-2399

March 3, 1997

Rick E. Wolfert
President & CEO
Keycorp Leasing Ltd.
54 State Street
Albany, NY 12201-0655

Dear Mr. Wolfert:

With more than 15 years of top-flight marketing experience in banking, financing and leasing, I know the business inside out. I know the business development techniques that work best. Most significantly, I have consistently outpaced the competition, won dominant positioning and delivered multi-million dollar growth.

Further, my expertise includes:

- Development of strategic marketing plans and their successful translation into tactical business development initiatives nationwide.

- Leadership of successful market research programs that provide relevant and factual data upon which to build successful market outreach and new business strategies.

- Conceptualization and development of product enhancements to expand market presence and drive sustained revenue growth.

- Development of high-impact, high-yield marketing communications programs.

- Creation of CD-ROM and other multimedia marketing and sales presentation tools.

If action, performance and results are your objectives, we should talk. I am ready for a new career challenge, and am confident that the strength of my marketing, business development and general management performance will be of significant value to your organization.

Sincerely,

Samuel P. Robinson

Enclosure

ARTHUR PATTERSON
9834 Plains Avenue
St. Louis, Missouri 60054
(607) 564-6412

September 21, 1997

Robert Dodson
3049 Alamo Circle
San Antonio, TX 89743

Dear Bob:

It has been a while since we've been in touch and I wanted to update you on my activities since resigning my position as President & CEO of Missouri Federal Bank.

Approached by Midwest Financial Services last year, I accepted an interim assignment to spearhead feasibility analysis and development of a multi-million dollar technology project. This has been a great opportunity to strengthen my skills in advanced information, networking and communications technology.

However, I miss the dynamics of my past executive position where I held full P&L, operating, marketing and regulatory responsibility for Tracy's entire organization. So ... I need your help!

Just beginning my search for a new executive position, I was hoping that you could perhaps offer some ideas, referrals and/or recommendations. My goal is a senior-level assignment within the financial services industry, either with a start-up venture, turnaround or high-growth organization. I am open to relocation virtually anywhere in the U.S. where the opportunity is right and the challenges are significant.

If you can offer any recommendations or contacts you feel would be of some advantage in my search process, it would be most appreciated. Knowing the complexity of our industry and the tremendous competition within the executive ranks, I'm hoping to get somewhat of an edge through your assistance.

I've enclosed my resume just to familiarize you with my career track and performance, and would be pleased to provide any additional information at your request. If, in the future, I can be of any assistance in your career management efforts, I would be delighted to reciprocate. Thank you.

Sincerely,

Arthur Patterson

Enclosure

WALTER H. CHRISTOPHSON
125 Pembroke Drive
Richmond, Virginia 25841

Home: (804) 253-2467

Office: (804) 727-0707

October 31, 1997

Jason Adler
Chairman
Fidelity Savings Bank
3942 Northeast 34th Street
Richmond, VA 25465

Dear Mr. Adler:

The dynamics of banking have changed so dramatically throughout my 20-year career that I often wonder if I really do work in the same industry!

With the tremendous regulatory changes, transition from "old-line" banking to customer service-driven organizations, and the unprecedented number of mergers and acquisitions, the challenges have been demanding. The latter has been most relevant to my career, having not only "survived" three major acquisitions, but playing a vital role in the integration of diverse operations, services, products and personnel.

Further, my achievements have included several successful business and product line start-ups, a number of aggressive reengineering and process redesign initiatives, and a constant focus on productivity, quality and financial gains. I am a strong operations manager, able to direct large staffs at multiple locations in the design and delivery of complete banking services to both corporate and consumer markets.

My financial results speak for themselves with recent achievements including:

* $7 million increase in new business volume through expanded marketing and direct sales initiatives.
* 30% gain in profit and revenue results despite near 50% workforce downsizing.
* Ranking in Gallup's Top 3% on customer service benchmarks.

After a successful effort in private consulting, I am anxious to return to the banking industry and look forward to speaking with you to explore management opportunities with Central Fidelity Bank. Thank you.

Sincerely,

Walter H. Christophson

Enclosure

NEAL DOUGLAS
13458 S.W. 62nd Street
Portland, Oregon 96542
(801) 386-7991

August 19, 1997

Allison Hentges
Director of Human Resources
National Bank of America, Inc.
9349 Fifth Avenue, 34th Floor
New York, NY 10031

Dear Ms. Hentges:

I am a well-qualified Banking Professional recognized for my expertise in solving operating problems, improving customer relations, accelerating fee income and asset growth, and strengthening personnel performance. Despite the many competitive challenges of our industry, I have consistently delivered results.

- **If your goal is to increase lending volume**, I originated over $1 million in mortgages within less than two years.

- **If your goal is to increase deposit growth**, I captured $8.8 million in net deposits in 1995.

- **If your goal is to strengthen your market position and customer image** I led a number of marketing, business development and outreach programs which dominated local markets and outperformed our competition.

- **If your goal is to enhance customer service**, I spearheaded a number of successful programs that not only increased customer satisfaction, but improved staff's focus on service, retention and performance.

My goal is to secure a management position with a leading financial institution seeking qualified, career-oriented professionals looking for long-term opportunities for employment and promotion. Thus my interest in meeting with you to explore such positions with your bank.

I appreciate your consideration and look forward to what I anticipate will be the first of many positive communications. Thank you.

Sincerely,

Neal Douglas

Enclosure

CONSTRUCTION

KeyWords, Action Verbs & High-Impact Phrases

To "Nail" Your Cover Letter:

* Project Planning, Administration & Management

* Large Dollar & Major Projects

* Regulatory Compliance & Reporting

* Environmental Issues & Hazardous Site Remediation

* Contract & Partner Negotiations

* Union & Trade Relations

* Investor Negotiations & Reporting

* Project Scheduling & Crewing

* Resource & Equipment Management

* Project Lifecycle Management

ERIC DOUGLAS
11249 Taylor Drive
Los Altos, California 94021

Home (415) 531-9492   Office (415) 529-3633

November 15, 1997

Michael Perry
Partner
Bastion Capital Corporation
972 Vallejo Street
Newport Beach, CA 92660

Dear Mr. Perry:

I am a well-qualified Construction Manager with extensive experience in the planning, staffing, budgeting and on-site field supervision of both new construction and renovation projects. With a total of 17 years' experience in construction and corporate facilities management, I bring to Bastion excellent skills in:

* All major construction trades including HVAC, electrical, roofing, framing, concrete forming and finishing, carpentry, ceramic tile and painting.

* Evaluating project costs and developing accurate project budgets.

* Selecting, negotiating contracts with and managing project subcontractors.

* Managing projects as per state and local building codes and regulations.

Most significant is my success in delivering projects on-time and within budget, despite the many challenges often encountered in the field. I have accomplished this through my ability to effectively plan, schedule and prioritize.

Currently working as a General Contractor, I have completed more than 15 projects in the past two years. Now, however, I am seeking to transition my experience back into a corporate environment and would welcome the opportunity for a personal interview to explore your need for talented, decisive and strong field leadership.

I appreciate your consideration and look forward to speaking with you. Thank you.

Sincerely,

Eric Douglas

Enclosure

EDWARD BRENTWOOD

5647 Chapel Drive
New Orleans, Louisiana 43241
(971) 984-3413

March 16, 1997

Bradley Majors
United Development Corp
11540 Santa Monica Boulevard, Suite 643
Los Angeles, CA 90021

Dear Mr. Majors:

Throughout my real estate development and construction management career, I have planned, designed, built and marketed more than 50 residential, commercial, health care, technology and light industrial properties worldwide. Total project values within the past 10 years have exceeded $450 million and served as the catalyst for large-scale inner city redevelopment as well as new community development projects.

Critical to my success is my ability to build cooperation among diverse public and private interests groups to fund and support project development. This has often required sensitive negotiations and communications, allowing me to rally support and drive forward projects with significant community and commercial impact.

Equally significant is my expertise in facilities management, maintenance and renovation. With responsibility for up to 35 properties, staffs of more than 200 and annual operating budgets of $15 + million, I have delivered strong performance results, reduced annual facilities costs and improved functional capabilities.

Currently, I am exploring new professional challenges and opportunities and will call to schedule an interview. Thank you.

Sincerely,

Edward Brentwood

Enclosure

CONSULTING

KeyWords, Action Verbs & High-Impact Phrases

To "Nail" Your Cover Letter:

* Project Planning & Execution

* Major Projects & Quantifiable Results

* Major Clients (*if not confidential*)

* Operations Turnaround

* Quality, Efficiency & Productivity Improvements

* Interim Executive Positions

* Client Presentations & Contract Negotiations

* Marketing & New Business Development

* Matrix Management & Team Leadership

* Performance Reengineering & Change Management

BARRY YOUNG

5421 Duplin Drive
Greensboro, North Carolina 27242

Home (910) 927-4510

Voice Mail (910) 342-9907

May 26, 1997

William C. Jones
Managing Partner
International Consultants, Inc.
3145 Seaview Avenue
Myrtle Beach, SC 28742

Dear Mr. Jones:

I am writing and forwarding my resume in anticipation that you may be interested in a well-qualified Senior Finance Executive to join your consulting team. My goal is to transition from the private sector into a high-profile consulting position where I can continue to provide strategic, transactions and financial management expertise.

Although I have worked within a large corporation, my career path has been unique, often as an internal consultant, advisor and special projects manager for several of the organization's largest subsidiaries. My focus has included start-up ventures, aggressive turnarounds and several high-growth, high-yield organizations. Highlights include:

* **Capital Financing**. Active participation in the 1994 $1 billion IPO of Malvern Materials.

* **Turnaround Management**. Leadership of a cross-functional reengineering team that saved the Information Systems Group $13 in annual operating costs while capturing $650 million in new business.

* **Technology Advancement**. Introduction of leading edge PC technologies to automate core business functions for Electronic Naval Systems Group.

* **Financial Analysis**. Design of strategic and tactical financial modeling and budgeting methodologies for the $1 billion Astronautics Group.

Most notable has been my success in building partnerships with senior management executives, operating personnel, outside advisors and consultants. Further, I have demonstrated my flexibility, moving from one business group to another, quickly evaluating their specific requirements, and initiating the appropriate course of action.

On a personal note, I bring to International Consultants well-developed problem solving, decision making, negotiation and project management skills, each of which I believe critical to a successful consulting career. I look forward to speaking with you and further investigating opportunities with your firm. Thank you.

Sincerely,

Barry Young

Enclosure

LAWRENCE NOLAN

3224 Malvern Drive
Pittsburgh, Pennsylvania 16532
(412) 396-2487

April 10, 1997

Mr. Steven Chappel
Global Technology Partners
349 Market Street
Philadelphia, PA 19601

Dear Mr. Chappel:

Although "technically" an employee, I have functioned as a consultant throughout the Westinghouse organization for more than 15 years. Working in a number of the company's operating divisions, my roles have ranged dramatically, from direct P&L responsibility for multi-site manufacturing operations to leadership of large-scale quality and business performance improvement initiatives. To each, I have contributed to measurable gains in revenues, profits and ROI.

My expertise lies in my ability to quickly and accurately assess a situation. What does each organization need in order to produce more, save money, increase earnings and strengthen its competitive position? These have been the challenges I have faced and the results I have delivered.

Currently, I am exploring the possibility for transitioning into a full-time consulting position specializing in quality, performance reengineering and/or operations. I believe the value of my experience — across broad industries, markets and functional disciplines — allows me to bring a unique perspective to your clients. More importantly, I will deliver results.

Please note that my strengths also include strategic planning, financial and operations analysis, team building and leadership, change management, process redesign, and executive presentations. I am direct and decisive in my leadership style, yet flexible in responding to constantly changing organizational, financial, operating and market demands.

I would welcome a personal interview to explore senior consulting opportunities and thank you for your time.

Sincerely,

Lawrence Nolan

Enclosure

RICHARD O'CONNOR
934 South Pearson Lane
Carmel, Indiana 45655
(404) 303-4398

January 17, 1997

Clifford Davis
Davis Consulting
1029 Brookline Drive
Indianapolis, IN 46731

Dear Mr. Davis:

Sometimes a fresh perspective, new strategies or an objective viewpoint are what's needed. When you're in the thick of the decision-making process, it is often difficult to "pull back" and identify what the best tactics are and how to accelerate your earnings.

This is the expertise I bring to an organization — my ability to quickly assess, evaluate, plan and initiate action. Whether challenged to launch a new technology venture, orchestrate the turnaround of an international business unit, or accelerate growth for an established technology leader, I have delivered strong financial results:

* 50%+ increase in ROI for ABC Technology Corporation.
* 35% increase in pre-tax profits for Australian Operations.
* 500% revenue growth for start-up turnkey systems supplier.
* $10 million revenue gain for one of IBM's largest reseller organizations.

Now, after a successful "corporate" career, I am interested in transitioning into the consulting arena where I can provide strong and decisive operating, marketing and/or development expertise. As such, my interest in your practice and request for a personal interview.

I will phone next week to follow-up and look forward to meeting with you.

Sincerely,

Richard O'Connor

Enclosure

DOMINION CONSULTING
Management, Operating & Marketing Solutions
230195 Pine Street Marketplace
Seattle, Washington 90641
Phone: (206) 496-0809
Email: dominion@msn.com

March 12, 1997

George Bergman
President
Impact Technology Manufacturing, Inc.
9394 Industrial Zone
Kent, WA 98321

Dear Mr. Bergman:

Are you struggling with core issues impacting the operation, revenues and profitability of your organization?

Are you in the midst of a start-up or emerging growth situation?

Are you spearheading an organization-wide reengineering and revitalization program?

Are you constantly evaluating all of your options to determine the most appropriate course of action?

Are you ready to make the next move?

Let Dominion Consulting help. With more than 20 years of top-flight executive management experience with Microsoft, Fujitsu, Xerox, Control Data and several emerging technology ventures, I have delivered consistently strong performance results. At each organization, my contributions positively impacted operations and financial performance.

My expertise spans virtually all core management functions with particular emphasis in worldwide sales and marketing, product management, multichannel distribution, manufacturing/operations, and organizational change/ performance improvement.

Today, I am the principal of Dominion Consulting, a unique, performance-driven consulting practice working exclusively with firms in the information technology and telecommunications industries to solve problems, meet challenges and improve financial results.

Let's take a few minutes to explore the challenges you are facing and your need for strong, decisive and immediate project leadership. I am available at your request for a free consultation.

Sincerely,

Timothy Lee, President

Enclosure

PATRICK M. DOUGHERTY
2492 Mission Road
Raleigh, North Carolina 24579

Phone (919) 282-6863   Fax (919) 286-0941

March 2, 1997

Thomas Wilder
Turnaround Consultants International
9845 Research Triangle
Raleigh, NC 27653

Dear Mr. Wilder:

As Acting CEO of a complex turnaround venture in the multimedia and broadcast industries, I am currently leading an aggressive reorganization, capital financing and market repositioning. My goal is to return the company to profitability within the first 12 months and position for long-term growth and diversification.

Previously, during my affiliation with Apple, Greene & West Co. (a well-respected turnaround management consulting group), I participated in several successful turnaround projects. My contributions were varied but focused on evaluating the feasibility of continued operations and how to redesign each organization for financial and operational revitalization.

Equally significant were my contributions to the successful turnaround of CCS Manufacturing. The company was faced with tremendous operating and financial challenges. Through the efforts of myself, the other executives and the entire workforce, we were able to reverse previous losses, lower corporate debt and enhance internal operating competencies.

My goal is to affiliate with a consulting and/or turnaround management organization seeking senior-level financial and operating leadership. I enjoy the challenges of turnaround situations and the opportunity to make immediate and substantive improvements.

I would, of course, be interested in pursuing any other opportunities you feel appropriate to my experience in not only turnaround management, but also start-up, emerging growth and high-growth ventures. Thank you.

Sincerely,

Patrick M. Dougherty

Enclosure

JAMES H. MARTIN
4595 Birch Street
Knoxville, Tennessee 54453
(935) 647-3214

November 15, 1997

Michael P. Charles
Charles Interim Executives
7953 Ivanhoe Avenue
Colorado Springs, CO 80632

Dear Mr. Charles:

Delivering value to client organizations has been the focus of my career for the past 12 years. With more than 100 completed engagements, I have consistently provided my clients with strategies, action plans and leadership critical to performance improvement, revenue and profit growth, cost reduction and technology gain. Most notably, I:

- Guided Capital Enterprises in the development of their marketing and business plans, and led a successful effort to raise $5 million in start-up funding.

- Delivered a $1+ million operating cost savings to James Berglund & Sons through consolidation of multiple plant facilities into one centralized operation.

- Negotiated joint venture, built to $4+ million in revenues and sold for 100% ROI.

- Spearheaded product development, manufacturing process reengineering and operations planning efforts (emphasis in technological, pharmaceutical and medical device industries).

- Pioneered innovative global sales, marketing and business development initiatives for key corporate clients.

I enjoy the "project challenge" and the dynamics of diverse corporate cultures. I excel in building new client relationships and managing cross-functional project teams. My leadership style is direct and decisive, yet I am able to maintain the flexibility critical to successful consulting and long-term client retention.

I would welcome the opportunity to pursue senior-level consulting opportunities and appreciate your consideration. I'll phone next week to schedule an interview. Thank you.

Sincerely,

James H. Martin

Enclosure

RAYMOND NICHOLAS
6417 Peakland Drive
Trenton, New Jersey 07585
(908) 721-5417

July 30, 1997

Joseph Binkley
Babcock, Binkley & Brown
9348 Henry Ford Highway
Detroit, MI 43573

Dear Mr. Binkley:

I am a well-qualified Senior Business and Financial Executive with more than 15 years experience. My goal is to transition my expertise from a corporate setting into the consulting arena where I can provide decisive operating leadership designed to improve processes, reduce costs, enhance technologies and improve net profit margins.

As you review my qualifications, you will note that I have progressed rapidly throughout a series of increasingly responsible management positions in a diversity of business markets — from advanced technology to industrial manufacturing to retail mass merchandising. Clearly, I have demonstrated my proficiency in translating business and financial processes from one industry to another, capitalizing upon core competencies to accelerate growth and performance improvement.

Throughout my career, I have acted as an internal consultant to boards of directors, executive teams and operating management to assist in strategic planning, corporate development, business process reengineering, quality gains, MIS acquisitions and crisis management. Just as significant is the strength of my experience in both domestic and international markets worldwide.

Recognized for my expertise in problem solving and turnaround management, I have delivered significant financial results within challenging organizations. However, I am not limited to turnaround management, and in fact, have managed new business unit start-ups, accelerated growth and well-established organizations.

I would welcome the opportunity to meet with you to explore consulting opportunities and appreciate both your time and consideration. I will phone next week to schedule a mutually convenient time. Thank you.

Sincerely,

Raymond Nicholas

Enclosure

CORPORATE DEVELOPMENT

KeyWords, Action Verbs & High-Impact Phrases

To "Nail" Your Cover Letter:

* Strategic Planning & Development

* Mergers & Acquisitions

* High-Profile Dealmaking & Transactions

* Joint Ventures & Strategic Alliances

* IPOs & Secondary Offerings

* Marketing & New Business Development

* Investor, Bank & Venture Capital "Road Shows"

* Financial Analysis & Projections

* Technology/Product Transfers & Licensing

* Revenue & Profit Growth

JOHN CARSON

2914 Lake Circle
Lexington, Kentucky 35643

Phone (230) 843-6548

Fax (230) 843-2380

May 1, 1997

John Glenn
President
Ceramitec, Inc.
Cincinnati, OH 65432

Dear Mr. Glenn:

With 18 years of senior-level corporate development experience in the materials industry, I bring to Ceramitec a strong record of revenue and earnings growth within highly competitive U.S. and global business markets. Most notably, I:

* Built Bondsil Corporation to over $15 million in revenue and spearheaded the development of customer, partner and co-producer relationships throughout the U.S., Europe and the Pacific Rim.

* Negotiated several acquisitions and international trading partnerships to accelerate Meyer's expansion throughout the U.S., Far East and Australian markets.

* Orchestrated the successful turnaround and return to profitability of Fulcrum through effective leadership of new business start-ups, product licensing programs, global joint ventures and other market-driven development efforts.

* Spearheaded Genstar's aggressive business development, acquisition, joint venture, partnership and marketing programs as the company grew from less than $6 million to over $33 million in revenues.

My greatest contribution to each of these companies — and others — has been my success in identifying and capitalizing upon market opportunities. Whether negotiating a joint venture to penetrate the Japanese market, structuring international co-producer agreements, or managing investment financing for an IPO, I have delivered strong financial and operating results.

I would welcome the opportunity to explore executive-level business development opportunities and appreciate your time in reviewing my qualifications. Be assured that my experience, network of contacts and product expertise within our industry will add measurable value to Ceramitec.

Sincerely,

John Carson

Enclosure

RICHARD FROST
663 Montgomery Street
Nashua, NH 06846
(601) 654-0417

October 3, 1997

Bruce McNaughton
President & CEO
McNaughton Holdings, LLC
934 Olympic Park Circle, Suite 647
Atlanta, GA 30542

Dear Mr. McNaughton:

I am a deal-maker with a unique expertise in corporate development, mergers, acquisitions and corporate financing. My strength lies in my ability to identify prime opportunities and drive forward complex due diligence, transactions and negotiations.

Throughout my tenure with Central Inc., I led the corporation's aggressive expansion program, managing 28 acquisitions and more than $90 million in corporate financings. In cooperation with the president of the company, we created a $110 million national organization from its infancy into what is now one of the largest and most successful organizations within the industry.

Equally notable are my accomplishments in general corporate financial affairs, strategic planning, MIS operations, business process redesign and team building/leadership. Each of these functions has contributed to the growth of the corporation by building a strong infrastructure to support our acquisition and expansion initiatives.

My goal is a top-flight corporate development position with an organization poised for aggressive market growth. I bring to McNaughton Holdings both the transactions and financial expertise critical to profitable, sustained and long-term development.

I look forward to meeting with you to explore opportunities and appreciate your consideration. Thank you.

Sincerely,

Richard Frost

Enclosure

TERRENCE JACKSON
5140 Avenida Las Cruces
Ft. Lauderdale, Florida 35302

Residence (954) 475-7188   Business (954) 594-6000 x254

December 12, 1997

Douglas Hall
Corporate Development, Inc.
9405 South Westwood Boulevard
Palo Alto, CA 96332

Dear Mr. Hall:

With over 10 years of senior-level management experience, I bring to Corporate Development substantial experience in the strategic planning and leadership of high-profile business development programs worldwide. Most notably, I:

- Structured, negotiated and transacted two major software company acquisitions with total annual revenues of more than $40 million.

- Integrated one of the above acquisitions with a prior acquisition to create a new, $54 million strategic business unit. As the SBU's Acting General Manager for a period of one year, I orchestrated the entire integration, realigned sales and marketing channels, developed 3-year strategic plan, and positioned for long-term, global market growth. Most significantly, I drove revenue growth by 28% within the first year.

- Participated in eight other acquisitions and eight divestitures, working to create a new organization offering products, technologies and services throughout established and emerging markets worldwide.

- Spearheaded more than 10 new product/new technology development projects, including the company's single largest development initiative ever (in cooperation with Microsoft).

Please note that in addition to the above projects and achievements, I have guided the development and positioning of global marketing programs that have further strengthened our market presence and bottom-line financial performance. Equally significant is my performance in strategic planning, finance, partner development and complex negotiations.

Currently I am employed as VP of Engineering with Dublin. My challenge to is create the corporation's first-ever engineering organization. To date, I have built a team of 45 top-producing engineering professionals and delivered over $22 million in new product revenues. However, I miss the dynamics and the excitement of the M&A process and am looking forward to returning to such a position as Director of Acquisitions for Corporate Development.

Sincerely,

Terrence Jackson

Enclosure

70

WILLIAM DUNN
945 Red Desert Circle
Santa Fe, New Mexico 87505
(505) 992-3522

September 23, 1997

David Rosenberg
President
TriStar Video
934 Paramount Drive
Los Angeles, CA 90032

Dear Mr. Rosenberg:

It is unique in today's marketplace to find an individual with a strong blend of financial management, operating management and creative expertise. It has often been my experience that the financial and executive decision-makers in the film and video production industry sit opposed to the creative talents. Objectives vary widely and communication is often strained.

My expertise is that I span that gap.

While negotiating over $270 million in investment and financing deals for my real estate asset management firm, I also was Executive Producer of a full-length feature film. One moment I was the "deal maker" and advisor to legal counsel on the formation of limited partnerships for specific real estate acquisitions; the next, I was reviewing scripts, selecting acting and creative design talent, and supervising daily film production operations.

That is the value I bring to TriStar. I can "sit on both sides of the fence" to evaluate proposed projects, structure complex financing transactions, manage daily business operations and facilitate cooperative efforts with writers, producers, actors and directors. With more than 20 years of top-flight entrepreneurial and executive management experience, I have demonstrated my ability to bring projects together and deliver results.

My personal interests in film and video production extend back to my teenage years. I am experienced in digital editing and have begun to build an extensive network of industry contacts. Now my goal is to merge my entrepreneurial, financial and creative talents to bring value and strong leadership to a well-established production company.

I would welcome the chance to pursue such opportunities with TriStar and appreciate your time and consideration. Thank you.

Sincerely,

William Dunn

Enclosure

ENERGY & ENVIRONMENTAL

KeyWords, Action Verbs & High-Impact Phrases

To "Nail" Your Cover Letter:

*   Environmental & Engineering Project Management

*   Regulatory Affairs & Compliance

*   Energy Generation & Cogeneration Projects

*   Site Remediation & Hazardous Materials Management

*   Resource Recovery & Conservation

*   Systems & Technologies

*   Public, Private & Institutional Funding

*   Cost Reduction & Avoidance

*   Joint Ventures, Strategic Alliances & Partnerships

*   Marketing, Business Development & Revenue Growth

LESLIE HOBBS
9024 Garden Circle
Dallas, Texas 41835
(201) 694-2958

November 11, 1997

Harry DeCovey
President
Indosuez Development International
600 Anton Boulevard, Suite 2393
Inglewood, CA 90301

Dear Mr. DeCovey:

The challenge during my career with FLAG was to build a sophisticated environmental management organization responsible for regulatory affairs, site remediation, hazardous materials management and legislative advocacy. Today, FLAG boasts of one of the most dynamic environmental organizations in the world, a pioneer in compliance, safety and risk management.

My contributions have been notable and include:

* Over $20 million in revenues and state funding through efforts in containment, cost recovery and cost avoidance.

* Dramatic reduction in the exposure and potential environmental liability of FLAG.

* Participation with other Fortune 500 companies (principally manufacturing, utilities and transportation) in the development of a common vision and action for environmental protection.

* Introduction of quantifiable performance measures to guide environmental initiatives.

Now, at this juncture in my career, I am seeking a top-level environmental management position with a leading manufacturer. The strength of my field experience and regulatory knowledge places me in a uniquely qualified position to make an immediate impact upon your environmental affairs.

I appreciate your time and will follow up next week. Thank you.

Sincerely,

Leslie Hobbs

Enclosure

WILLIAM D. SMITH
1915 St. Cloud Drive
Orlando, Florida 33653
(561) 352-6564

February 13, 1997

Jonathan Boman
Chairman of the Board
Innocal Environmental
9345 SW 98th Avenue
Miami, FL 33874

Dear Mr. Boman:

Throughout the past 10 years, I have been a driving force in transitioning Cirrus from a domestic energy company into a diversified multinational corporation with successful ventures throughout Australia, the Far East and Latin America. Challenged by the board to identify and capitalize upon international opportunities, I provided corporate development, financing and negotiations expertise that catapulted Cirrus into a $2 billion organization.

Most notable are my successes in building start-up ventures, orchestrating complex turnarounds of international corporations and accelerating growth within established entities. Further, I have structured and negotiated complex joint ventures and partnerships worldwide to expand market presence, drive revenue growth and strengthen corporate earnings.

My resume highlights specific projects and achievements, ranging from negotiation of international debt financings and foreign hedging programs to creation of innovative marketing and business development strategies. Each has delivered strong and sustainable gains in corporate value — to our customers, our operations and our shareholders.

Now, at this juncture in my career, I am seeking new challenges where I can continue to provide leadership for sophisticated financial transactions, corporate reorganizations and global development projects. I guarantee improved financial results and look forward to exploring opportunities with your organization.

Sincerely,

William D. Smith

Enclosure

74

FLOYD P. FISHER

2394 Michigan Avenue
Chicago, Illinois 60124

Home (847) 255-9188
Office (847) 968-5402
Email   123@net.com

July 23, 1997

Douglas Carter
President
Zulandi Kyocera, Inc.
1055 Oakton Avenue
Chicago, IL 60012

Dear Mr. Carter:

Building asset value and accelerating cash flow are my expertise. With more than 15 years of senior-level development experience in the energy/utility industry, I have negotiated projects world-wide that have generated cumulative earnings of more than $400 million and positioned MG&G as a dominant player in the international development industry.

Starting with a concept in early 1987, the President and I have created one of the most well-respected and fastest growing companies in the industry. To my credit are the significant deals and projects we have negotiated, establishing our presence on five continents and in more than 25 countries.

Not only have I developed successful new ventures, I have repeatedly demonstrated my success in M&A transactions, corporate financing and strategic diversification. I am goal-directed and results-driven with strong and decisive leadership skills. Most important, I am a negotiator, able to facilitate consensus and deliver profit to all partners.

At this point in my career I am seeking new challenges within the power industry and would welcome the chance to pursue any appropriate opportunities with your client companies. I am interested in a senior level operating management position with either domestic and/or international responsibilities. I am open to relocation and would be delighted to discuss compensation requirements at your convenience.

Sincerely,

Floyd P. Fisher

Enclosure

ENGINEERING

KeyWords, Action Verbs & High-Impact Phrases

To "Nail" Your Cover Letter:

* New Product & Technology Development

* Cross-Functional Team Leadership

* Quality Assurance & TQM Initiatives

* Process Development

* Budget & Cost Improvements

* Sales & Marketing Contributions

* Information Systems & Automation

* Marketing & Resource Management

* Joint Venture & Partnership Projects

* Time-to-Market Improvements

FRANK MILANOVICH
934 Old State Road
Albany, New York 19510
(914) 719-5483

October 24, 1997

William Vanderbilt
President & CEO
The Vanderbilt Group
934 Avenue of the Americas, 12th Floor
New York, New York 10013

Dear Mr. Vanderbilt:

Building organizational value is my expertise. As the Director of Corporate Engineering for Chromitec Corporation and its affiliate company, Boyd Chemical, I pioneered innovative engineering and operating solutions to improve productivity, reduce operating costs, enhance efficiencies and accelerate profit gains.

With more than 20 years experience, I bring to The Vanderbilt Group a strong track record of management and engineering performance:

- Leadership of more than $45 million in total capital improvement projects.

- Management of corporate engineering projects for both existing and start-up facilities in the U.S., Germany, France and The Netherlands.

- Training, development and leadership of 55+ multi-discipline engineering professionals.

- Expertise in all core operating, manufacturing, process and quality management methods.

- Direct P&L accountability for both projects and full-scale plant operations.

My goal is a senior-level management position with an organization in need of strong, decisive and proactive engineering leadership. I am open to relocation worldwide, speak five languages fluently and most significantly, have demonstrated my ability to impact positive change and strengthen profitability.

I look forward to speaking with you regarding appropriate opportunities and thank you in advance for your consideration. My salary requirements are flexible.

Sincerely,

Frank Milanovich

Enclosure

PAUL T. BANYAN
873 Joan Drive
Jasper, WY 83764
(222) 385-3726

January 5, 1997

Bob Bolt
Engineering Manager
Simpl-Mold, Inc.
898 Gray Weigh Station
Jasper, WY 83766

Dear Mr. Bolt:

I am writing at the suggestion of my father-in-law, John Lewis and would like to submit my resume for consideration for the position of Project Engineer as advertised in last week's Jasper Forum. I bring to the position:

- Nine years of experience in the design and engineering of large-scale industrial and manufacturing facilities, including both new facilities construction and large-scale renovation.

- Excellent skills in managing cross-functional design, engineering and project teams.

- Leadership of project scheduling, subcontracting and progress reporting.

- Control of up to $22 million in annual project budgets.

- Introduction of advanced PC technologies to automate and enhance engineering capabilities.

I bring to Simpl-Mold combined strengths in both "hands-on" engineering as well as project leadership. In turn, I guarantee my ability to meet project budget and scheduling objectives, deliver improved technologies and support your expanding operations.

Thank you. As requested, my salary requirements are $115,000+.

Sincerely,

Paul T. Banyan

Enclosure

KATHRYN M. HAMBRECHT
1915 Camden Circle
Cherry Hill, New Jersey 09648
Home (609) 970-3245   Office (609) 647-0359

December 1, 1997

Robert Carmickle
Director
Nuclear Testing, Inc.
1900 Industrial Way
Roswell, NM 54321

Dear Mr. Carmickle:

I am a well-qualified Environmental Engineer with 12 years' experience directing hazardous waste and site remediation programs nationwide. I bring to the Nuclear Testing broad industry experience, expert regulatory knowledge, and the ability to reduce your environmental costs and limit your exposure.

Highlights of my professional career that may be of particular interest to you include the following:

* Saved my current employer $1 million in potential remediation costs by identifying critical issues negating the value of proposed acquisitions and divestitures.

* Saved a large industrial manufacturer $650,000 in site remediation and hazardous materials disposal costs through well-planned, efficient and timely project management.

* Directed more than 100 Superfund remediation projects for the EPA.

My strengths lie in my ability to manage the entire process — from site review and analysis through planning, budgeting, engineering, field management and regulatory approval. Further, I have extensive experience in environmental training for both executive and operating teams.

Although secure in my current position, I am confidentially exploring new professional challenges and opportunities. Thus my interest in the Nuclear Testing and request for a personal interview. Thank you.

Sincerely,

Kathryn M. Hambrecht

Enclosure

CHRISTIAN LAMBERT
9348 Mississippi Street
Minneapolis, Minnesota 55321
606-535-6533

March 21, 1997

Abbott Laboratories
Job Code 96-MAO-GDM 1
1401 Sheridan Road
Dept. 39Y, A-1
North Chicago, IL 60064

RE: <u>Environmental Coordinator</u>

Dear Sir/Madam:

With 13 years of professional experience in Environmental Engineering, I bring to Abbott Laboratories an in-depth knowledge of environmental issues, regulations and compliance impacting chemical and industrial manufacturing. The scope of my responsibility has varied widely, from environmental review and analysis of proposed site acquisitions to comprehensive assessment of the waste by-products generated in large manufacturing operations.

Highlights of my career that may be of particular interest to you include:

- Expertise in resource recovery and conservation.
- Completion of 100+ Superfund projects.
- Extensive knowledge of soil, air and groundwater remediation systems and technologies.
- Design of environmental systems for hazardous waste, hazardous materials, air emissions and wastewater discharges.

Most significant has been my success in resolving long-standing environmental issues, achieving compliance with state and federal regulations, and reducing the costs associated with environmental engineering and remediation. Further, I have worked closely with senior management to guide their acquisition, divestiture, product development and other business development efforts.

Although currently employed, I am anxious to return to a manufacturing environment and would be delighted to have the opportunity to interview with Abbott Laboratories. I appreciate your confidentiality and look forward to speaking with you. My salary history and expectations can be discussed at the time of our interview. Thank you.

Sincerely,

Christian Lambert

Enclosure

LAWRENCE J. JUSTUS
73223 Lorado Road
Austin, Texas 73648
Phone (999) 391-3847   Fax (999) 391-3850

July 11, 1996

Metra Mellane
President & CEO
Mellane Industries
1836 Peekaboo Drive
Lester, Texas 73543

Dear Mr. Mellane:

In response to your advertisement for a Senior Engineering Manager - Chemical Industry, please note the following:

<u>Your Requirements</u>	<u>My Qualifications</u>
20+ Year Engineering Career	<u>22 years of experience in Chemical Engineering</u> -- from Bench Tech to Field Service Manager to Project Leader to Director of Chemical Products Design & Engineering.
Financial Expertise	Negotiation and administration of more than <u>$225 million in projects</u> over the past five years.
New Product Development	Leadership of design and engineering teams that delivered <u>over 35 new products</u> to markets worldwide for Ciba-Geigy and others.
Strong Leadership Skills	Management of <u>cross-functional teams</u> of design, engineering, consulting and manufacturing engineers working cooperatively on multi-million dollar development projects.
MBA & MS Degrees	<u>MBA</u> from Harvard; <u>MS - Chemical Eng</u>. from USC.

If your goals are action, results and improved financial performance, we should talk. In response to your request for salary history, I prefer to discuss my compensation at the time of an interview. Thank you.

Sincerely,

Lawrence J. Justus

Enclosure

81

FINANCE

KeyWords, Action Verbs & High-Impact Phrases

To "Nail" Your Cover Letter:

* Cost Reduction & Profit Improvement

* Information Systems Development & Implementation

* Investment, Acquisition & Capital Financings

* Corporate Administration

* Cost Accounting & General Accounting Processes

* Streamlining & Reengineering Projects

* Interest Fee & Cost Savings

* Debt Reduction Negotiations

* IPOs & Secondary Offerings

* High-Profile Contract Negotiations

Paul C. Scott

1839 Riversound Drive
Forest Lake, Minnesota 55173
612-333-9939

May 5, 1997

Steven L. Brown
President
LTI Technologies, Inc.
2727 Union Street
LaCrosse, WI 86324

Dear Mr. Brown:

As Chief Financial Officer for Data Management Systems, Inc., an emerging technology development venture, I was challenged to build a complete financial infrastructure to support the company as it transitioned from development through market launch. Understanding the market and attempting to "predict" its performance was critical in establishing our financial plans, cost management systems and projections.

Just as with other start-up ventures, Data Management needed initial funding and I was charged with preparing and completing a successful NASDAQ IPO. Despite the financing, the company is still facing some significant challenges, and I have decided to pursue opportunities elsewhere.

My objective is a senior-level Finance position with a small to midsize company in need of strong and decisive financial, operating and technological leadership. With 10+ years experience as CFO, VP of Finance and Corporate Treasurer, I have met the complex financial and operating challenges associated with start-up, turnaround, growth and multinational companies worldwide. Briefly summarized, my experience includes:

- All general corporate finance, accounting, treasury and controllership functions.
- Development and management of more than 25 mergers, acquisitions, divestitures, strategic alliances, LBOs, IPOs and joint ventures.
- Execution of $200+ million in public and private financings.
- Management of complex foreign currency, foreign exchange and international banking transactions.

I am limiting my search to Minnesota, Wisconsin and Nebraska. It is a region in which I have worked for years and have extensive professional contacts. As such, I would welcome a personal interview and appreciate your time and consideration. I will follow-up next week.

Sincerely,

Paul C. Scott

Enclosure

CATHERINE LANGHORNE
119 Stillwatch Circle
Garden City, New York 11564
(516) 653-6353

January 12, 1997

Rodney Chatney
President
Health Care Systems, Inc.
330 North Boulevard
San Diego, CA 92123

Dear Mr. Chatney:

During my tenure as CFO and Vice President/Corporate Controller of three uniquely different health care companies, I acquired tremendous experience within diverse health care service and technology markets throughout the U.S. and abroad. To each, I delivered strong operating and financial results despite often enormous market, regulatory and economic challenges. Most notably, I:

* **Recently completed a successful IPO** for an emerging health care technology company poised for tremendous market growth with the introduction of pioneering disease management systems.

* **Built the #1 business unit (Finance)** in United Health's worldwide operations. Received recognition based on operational gains, best practices and overall management performance.

* **Introduced sophisticated information technologies** to further automate and streamline accounting, billing, financial reporting and cash flow operations.

* Structured and negotiated complex business development initiatives including **public and private financings, mergers, acquisitions and joint ventures worldwide.**

The strength of my financial expertise is solid and encompasses all core financial and treasury affairs, financing and investment banking, merger and acquisition transactions, SEC affairs and large-scale administrative functions. Just as significant are my qualifications in business unit finance, budgeting, cost control, ABC accounting and other "hands-on" operations.

If you are interested in a strong, decisive and performance-driven Finance Executive, I am your candidate. My approach is that of proactive change, enabling organizations to grow, expand and diversify while improving profitability and strengthening operating performance.

Sincerely,

Catherine Langhorne

Enclosure

BERNARD PFEIFER

832 Westend Street
Watertown, New York 16452

Home   (818) 438-7971
Office   (818) 867-2010

September 1, 1997

Michael Caufield
Senior Vice President
Bayside Manufacturing, Inc.
1900 Commercial Way
Bayside, NY 11387

Dear Mr. Caufield:

Corporate finance is no longer just a "numbers" game. As the Senior Financial Manager with Merlena, my responsibilities have extended far beyond finance to include strategic and tactical business planning, marketing, new product development, MIS, sales administration, manufacturing and general operating management within several of the corporation's emerging and high-growth business units. Results have been significant:

- Financial leadership for development and market launch of three major product lines, subsequently generating over $30 million in new revenues to the corporation.
- Reorganization of core business function, delivering a 25% staff reduction with no loss in performance.
- Financial and operating oversight for PC system installations and upgrades to automate field sales and marketing organizations.
- Management of a dynamic $20+ million budgeting process impacting all major operating units throughout the corporation.
- Coordination of large-scale business operating plans with particular emphasis on financial, capital, marketing and organizational development components.

My management style is direct and decisive, yet flexible in responding to the constantly changing demands of my staff, management teams and the marketplace. Most significant is my ability to work across diverse divisions (e.g., sales, marketing, contracts, MIS, product development), linking finance with operations to facilitate expansion, reorganization and operating improvements.

Never satisfied with the "status quo," I earned a reputation throughout Merlena for not only the strength of my financial expertise, but for my ability to communicate and coordinate cooperative efforts through cross-functional business teams.

I look forward to speaking with you to further highlight my qualifications and explore your specific financial needs and operating objectives. Thank you.

Sincerely,

Bernard Pfeifer

Enclosure

BRUCE McGEE
3000 Sandhill Drive
Salt Lake City, Utah 75321
(653) 654-5437

August 1, 1997

Wayne Montgomery
Montgomery Executive Recruiters, Inc.
1010 Fifth Avenue
New York, NY 10010

Dear Mr. Montgomery:

I am writing and forwarding my resume in anticipation that you may be working with a client company seeking a market-driven Finance Executive with broad cross-functional experience in emerging, high-growth and well-established corporations. Unlike other financial managers, my focus has not been limited to just finance, but expanded to include coordination of sales, marketing, product development, strategic planning and performance improvement teams. Highlights of my career include:

* Fifteen years of top-level financial management experience with Gold Ford, Inc., providing strong and decisive leadership for diverse operating divisions and business units.

* Consistent record of achievement in reducing operating costs, improving profit contributions and strengthening operating performance.

* Financial and operating oversight for PC system installations and upgrades to automate field sales and marketing organizations.

* Strategic and tactical management support to strengthen operations, improve productivity and solidify market position.

In addition to my financial responsibilities, I have provided "hands-on" operating leadership in strategic planning, marketing, new product development, business process redesign, manufacturing, sales administration and other core operations. I am decisive in my leadership style, yet flexible in responding to the constantly changing demands of my staff, management team and the marketplace.

At this point in my career, I am seeking a top-level financial management position with a high-growth, turnaround and/or well-established corporation. I am flexible in my compensation requirements and willing to consider relocation for the right opportunity.

If you are working with a client company seeking action and improved financial results, we should talk. I appreciate your time and look forward to speaking with you.

Sincerely,

Bruce McGee

Enclosure

ALLEN MORGENSTERN

190 Salmon Road
White Plains, New York 10631
EMail: amorgen@att.net

Home: (591) 885-3389   Office: (591) 399-6400

April 15, 1997

Sidney G. Lawrence
President
Hedgerow, Inc.
1029 Seaside Road
Warwick, RI 02886

Dear Mr. Lawrence:

With 15+ years of top-flight Corporate Finance & Treasury Management expertise, I bring to your organization a strong record of financial, investment, operational and strategic performance. Most notably, I:

- Established two new and comprehensive corporate treasury operations for New Enterprise Services and Sea-Bass Corporation. Starting with virtually nothing, I built both organizations from ground floor into top-performing organizations successful in responding to the dynamic operating needs of each corporation.

- Structured and negotiated over $50 million in investment transactions, private placement, loans and corporate debt restructurings.

- Captured a total of $10 million in cost savings over the past eight years.

- Spearheaded selection and implementation of advanced MIS and PC technologies to automate all accounting, financial planning, financial reporting, investment and tax management operations.

- Reorganized core financial, administrative and operating functions for substantial cost reduction and performance improvement.

These achievements are indicative of the quality and caliber of my entire professional career — identify opportunities to strengthen financial affairs, reduce costs and improve support to operations worldwide.

Now, at this point in my career, I am seeking new executive opportunities where I can again build and lead a sophisticated financial and treasury organization. I look forward to a personal interview. Thank you.

Sincerely,

Allen Morgenstern

Enclosure

MICHELLE P. BAUER
1281 Lighthouse Circle
Boston, Massachusetts 08796
Home (954) 642-4140   Office (954) 652-5159

March 4, 1997

Box JJ-230
Wall Street Journal
1233 Regal Row
Dallas, Texas 75247

Dear Sir/Madam:

In need of a Director of Budgeting & Planning? Let me tell you why I'm the perfect candidate:

- 12 years of progressively responsible experience in corporate planning, budgeting, accounting and finance, advancing to my most recent positions as a Financial Controller and Financial Director with Pacific Regional, providing comprehensive financial leadership to up to 50 business units nationwide.

- Expert qualifications in financial planning and analysis, consolidated financial reporting, cost analysis, forecasting, cost reduction/avoidance, feasibility analysis, capital expenditures and internal audit.

- Design, development and implementation of comprehensive budgeting and strategic planning function.

- Success in linking finance with other core operating departments, transitioning finance from a "regulatory" function into a cooperative business partner responsive to constantly changing operating, market and financial demands.

- Extensive IS experience throughout my career with recent leadership responsibility (in cooperation with other management executives) for a multi-million dollar SAP implementation.

- Strategic and tactical financial leadership to top-level operating and management executives throughout the Pacific organization.

- MBA, CPA and CISA (Certified Information Systems Auditor) credentials.

Although secure in my current position, I am confidentially exploring new professional challenges and opportunities. Thus my interest in interviewing for the position of Director of Budgeting & Planning where I guarantee I can provide strong, decisive and results-driven financial leadership.

I appreciate your time in reviewing my qualifications and look forward to speaking with you.

Sincerely,

Michelle P. Bauer

Enclosure

NATHAN O'GRADY
985 Marketplace Circle
Newbury Falls, Montana 88838
(998) 324-6431

October 5, 1997

Rick Daly, President
Newtec International
LaGrangeville, NY 12540

Dear Mr. Daly:

As the Vice President of Finance, Chief Financial Officer and member of the Executive Management team of several U.S. and international corporations, I have earned an excellent reputation for my ability to provide strong and decisive operating leadership in challenging situations. I bring to Newtec International a unique blend of experience in general management, financial management, sales and marketing leadership, strategic planning, team building and technology. Most notably, I:

* Created the strategies, defined the action plans and led the successful turnaround of Gestpak's U.S. sales organization as a member of the executive team.
  RESULTS: 20% sales growth and 100%+ profit contribution.

* Developed integrated systems and financial controls for a start-up satellite communications company (joint venture between White Communications and Express, Inc.).
  RESULTS: 50% growth in two years.

* Restructured and automated operations in the U.S., Canada and Mexico for both Gestpak and Mobile.
  RESULTS: 15% operating expense reduction and 20% accounts receivable reduction.

* Led a complex restructuring of corporate debt and balance sheet for Mobile.
  RESULTS: Successful $80 million private securities placement, $50 million capital equipment financing arrangement, significant cash flow improvement and long-term debt reduction.

My greatest strength lies in my ability to identify opportunities — for cost savings, revenue growth, quality improvement and increased profitability. Just as significant has been my success in creating the strategic and tactical operating plans to capitalize upon these opportunities and deliver results.

I would welcome the chance to explore senior-level financial opportunities and appreciate your consideration. Be assured that the strength of my financial and operating experience will add measurable value to your organization.

Sincerely,

Nathan O'Grady

Enclosure

CONRAD P. JOHNSON

265 University Avenue
Philadelphia, Pennsylvania 19603
Email: cjohnson@prime.com

Home (872) 592-2339
Office (872) 345-8156
Fax (872) 345-8166

January 20, 1997

Alexander Washington
President
Peregrine, Inc.
150 West 9th Street
New York, NY 10025

Dear Mr. Washington:

For the past seven years, I have guided high-level strategic business planning and financial planning efforts on behalf of Prime Services, as the company grew from less than $2 million to over $80 million in annual revenues. My challenge was to identify and capitalize upon opportunities to expand market reach, drive revenue growth, reduce operating costs, and improve the overall productivity and performance of this dynamic organization.

Results have been significant. Not only has the company grown over the past several years, through my leadership, our marketing and business development efforts are more focused, our distribution channels are broader, our advertising base invests significantly higher dollars, and our customer retention rate is one of the best in the industry.

Equally significant is the strength of my financial planning, analysis and management skills. Beginning my professional career with several major industry players — Pfizer, Pitney Bowes & Savin — I quickly demonstrated my ability to "understand the numbers" and translate retrospective review into market-driven action. This skill set has been the single most critical factor in my success and leadership performance.

Now, at this point in my career, I am seeking new senior-level financial and business planning opportunities. Aware of your organization's performance and commitment to excellence, and in anticipation that you may be interested in a candidate with my qualifications, I have enclosed my resume and look forward to speaking with you.

Sincerely,

Conrad P. Johnson

Enclosure

PHILLIP CHAPMAN
109 South 114th Avenue
Kirkland, Washington 98332
(508) 336-9149

March 16, 1997

Franklin Woodrow
Vanguard Financial
1900 Bayou Lane
Baton Rouge, LA 70808

Dear Mr. Woodrow:

I am writing to express my interest in Financial Planning, Research & Analysis positions with Vanguard and have included my resume for your review. I am particularly interested in opportunities in the oil, gas and chemical industries where I have eight years of professional experience and an excellent knowledge of the economic, technological and production trends impacting the industry.

As you review my qualifications you will note that my career has involved a unique blend of analytical, financial, budgeting, project management and technical responsibilities, all focused on improving yield, increasing production and reducing operating costs. Beginning each project with an in-depth review of the technology involved, I then spearheaded complex operational and financial analyses to provide measurable baseline data to monitor and impact future performance.

The results of our efforts were significant and include multi-million dollar cost reductions, yield improvements and revenue/earnings gains.

Now, at this point in my career, I am seeking to transfer my knowledge into a finance position where I can continue to provide the research, analytical and industry knowledge critical to financial improvement and growth. Thus my interest in Vanguard and request for a personal interview.

Sincerely,

Phillip Chapman

Enclosure

MARTINA VANDERSLOOT
119 Central Park West, 4D
New York, New York 10025
Home (212) 867-9247

February 1, 1997

Human Resources Manager
The Museum of Modern Art
11 West 53 Street
New York, NY 10019

Dear Sir/Madam:

I've had a most unusual financial management career! And, I assume, you're looking for a most unusual and talented Project Director / Deputy Controller.

Let me tell you a bit about myself and my career. With Acction, Inc. since 1984, I have advanced rapidly, earned five major promotions, and am currently spearheading a large-scale project development initiative. More core competencies include:

- 13 years' experience in financial management, financial process, analytical methods and project management.

- Extensive qualifications in the design, development and introduction of advanced information systems technologies for both in-house and customer use.

- Expert skills in identifying organizational needs, analyzing opportunities, developing reporting protocols and spearheading business development initiatives.

- Excellent accounting, financial management, budgeting, cost management, cost/performance analysis and investment management experience. Familiar with FASB, GAAP and other industry regulations.

- Outstanding oral and written communication skills. Strong qualifications in team building and team leadership.

Although secure in my current position, I am confidentially exploring new professional challenges and opportunities to manage unique projects, programs and business units. As such, my interest in your search for a Project Director / Deputy Controller and request for a personal interview. As requested, my salary has averaged $150,000+ over the past several years. Thank you.

Sincerely,

Martina Vandersloot

Enclosure

FOOD & BEVERAGE

KeyWords, Action Verbs & High-Impact Phrases

To "Nail" Your Cover Letter:

* Labor Cost Savings

* Food Cost Controls

* Purchasing & Supplier Negotiations

* Menu Development & Profitable Pricing

* Productivity Improvement

* Guest Relations & Retention

* Staff Training & Development

* Multi-Site Operations Management

* New Site Start-Up

* Special Events

ELVIS P. CASCELLA

771 Ross Drive
Lawrence, Kansas 45434

Home (555) 978-8050
Fax (555) 978-0155

January 26, 1997

Coca-Cola Foods
Ad #96-C
P.O. Box 2079
Houston, TX 77252-2079

Dear Sir/Madam:

With more than 15 years' experience in Food Industry sales, marketing and business development programs, I bring to Coca-Cola Foods the exact qualifications you seek for the position of Region Market Manager.

- Expertise in identifying, developing and managing business development programs designed to penetrate emerging markets, accelerate growth within existing markets, and strengthen annual revenue performance.

- Extensive qualifications in the recruitment, training and leadership of both direct sales and broker sales networks.

- Strong strategic planning skills with proven success in translating strategy into tactical action plans.

- Delivery of multi-million dollar revenue growth within challenging and competitive business markets.

- Excellent record of performance in managing and further developing key account relationships with strong presentation, negotiation and sales closing skills.

Most significant is my ability to build and manage cooperative working relationships with my sales teams, distributors and customers. Through these efforts, we have been successful in launching new products, redefining our product mix to meet market demand, and outperforming competition.

After years of sales experience within the food service industry, I was recruited to accelerate a sales and marketing program for a national organization. Within the first year, I delivered significant revenue gains and strengthened our retention by 58%. Although successful, I miss the dynamics of the food service industry and am now pursuing opportunities to return. As such, my interest in your search and request for a personal interview.

Sincerely,

Elvis P. Cascella

Enclosure

HORACE RENE

1006 Avenue de Apartie
Montreal, Quebec H5P 3T1
Phone (514) 478-9825   Fax (514) 478-2148

December 1, 1997

Jacques Levesque
Director
Le Hotelier
1984 Noset Boulevard
Montreal, Quebec H9R 1Q9

Dear Mr. Levesque:

I have recently relocated to Montreal and am contacting you to express my interest in employment opportunities. With 15 years experience in the Food & Beverage industry, I offer:

* Excellent qualifications in the start-up of new F&B outlets, banquet operations and conference centers, as well as the expansion of existing service operations.

* Consistent achievement of all expense budgets and revenue objectives with strong analytical and negotiating skills.

* Demonstrated success in increasing customer satisfaction and retention, improving revenues and outperforming competition.

* Strong skills in recruiting, training and supervising a large service staff.

I have worked for properties around the world, many with exclusive F&B operations. To each, I have provided strong and effective management and improved financial gains. I realize, however, no matter the strength of my experience, relocation to a new country is always a challenge and requires a learning curve. I am ready for such a challenge and anxious to reignite my career.

I am available, of course, at your convenience for an interview and thank you in advance for your consideration.

Sincerely,

Horace Rene

Enclosure

HENRY MARTINEZ
119 Circle Court
Ocean City, New Jersey 19117
(609) 356-8919

November 15, 1997

Director of Operations
Caesar's Palace
2000 Flamingo Road
Las Vegas, NV 76532

Dear Sir/Madam:

I am a well-qualified Food & Beverage Professional with more than 10 years of top-flight management experience. Beginning my career with the Sands Hotel & Casino, I advanced through a series of positions from Cook to Supervisor to my final promotion as Assistant Manager of five operating locations. Subsequently I was recruited to lead a diversity of F&B operations within the entertainment, restaurant, hotel and contract food service industries.

Through my strengths in personnel management, budgeting, administration, quality assurance and purchasing, I have met and/or exceeded all operating challenges — to increase revenues, control costs, improve staff productivity and efficiency, and deliver strong and sustainable results in customer service, satisfaction and retention. I am creative and team-oriented in my leadership style. I expect top performance in myself and my staff, and strive to instill a sense of personal worth and contribution to achieve overall corporate goals.

Now, my goal is to return to the casino industry where I can again lead fast-paced, customer-driven operations. I am in the process of relocating to Las Vegas and would welcome a personal interview to explore management opportunities with Caesar's Palace. I look forward to what I hope are the first of many positive communications.

Sincerely,

Henry Martinez

Enclosure

GOVERNMENT

KeyWords, Action Verbs & High-Impact Phrases

To "Nail" Your Cover Letter:

* Financial Operations & Administrative Management

* Increased Budget Appropriations

* Policy & Procedure Development

* Regulatory & Legislative Compliance

* Constituent Development & Relations

* Consensus Building

* Contract Negotiations & Administration

* Public & Private Partnerships

* Municipal Service Operations

* Economic & Business Development Programs

WILLIAM J. FOX
28 Babbling Brook
Hartford, Connecticut 06987
(203) 692-2323

April 29, 1997

Personnel Policies Subcommittee
Legislative Office Building
Room 5100
Hartford, CT 06106-1591

RE: Executive Director Search

Dear Sir/Madam:

Throughout my 14-year career in Municipal & Legislative Management, I have not only demonstrated strong business management qualifications, but the unique ability to build consensus among diverse political and special interest groups to work cooperatively towards common goals. The combination of both has been the foundation for my success and my contributions.

As you review my resume, you will note that I bring a strong portfolio of general management skills to the General Assembly. Most significant is my expertise in finance, budgeting, human resources, contracts, facilities management, administration and information technology. Further, I have been personally accountable for legislative reporting and regulatory compliance for three large municipalities throughout the Eastern U.S.

My greatest value to General Assembly is my professional network. Active in municipal and statewide legislative affairs for the past several years, I have built strong working relationships with legislative and judicial leaders throughout the state. These relationships will inevitably be of significant value in my ability to manage within the Assembly.

I am anxious to interview for the position and will follow-up next week. Salary is negotiable. Thank you.

Sincerely,

William J. Fox

Enclosure

98

MATTHEW P. WEBSTER
20 Clayton Court
San Diego, California 95174

Phone (415) 672-1030   Fax (415) 672-1012

October 20, 1997

Robert Dickstein
President
AT&T, Inc.
1500 Edison Avenue
New York, NY 10010

Dear Mr. Dickstein:

With more than 15 years' experience in the Telecommunications Industry, I bring to AT&T a unique expertise in Right of Way Operations and Government Affairs. Currently, as the Director of Local Government Relations for my company's largest-ever technology deployment, I am leading a highly-visible initiative to win the support of local municipalities to facilitate our projects and further our competitive position within the market.

Previously, during my tenure as Right of Way Manager, I led the management team that structured and negotiated hundreds of easements to support our expansion and regional diversification. This position also required extensive government liaison efforts to meet our immediate and long-term objectives.

My greatest strength lies in my ability to build consensus. I have been recognized throughout my career for consistent success in team building and project success. Further, I have broad technical, engineering and legal qualifications specific to the telecommunications industry (including wireless video and other emerging technologies).

Although secure in my current position, I have decided to pursue new professional challenges and would welcome the opportunity for a personal interview at your convenience. I appreciate your confidentiality and look forward to speaking with you.

Sincerely,

Matthew P. Webster

Enclosure

JEFFERY A. CAVANAUGH
1928 Woodland Drive
Charlotte, North Carolina 28213
(704) 523-0609

September 5, 1997

Robert O'Connor
Commissioner, City of Sacramento
P.O. Box 1090
Sacramento, CA 98231-1090

Dear Mr. O'Connor:

For the past 14 years, I have held several increasingly responsible positions as Finance Commissioner / Finance Director for three large municipal government organizations. To each city, I have provided strong and decisive financial leadership, delivered tremendous financial gains, and positioned for long-term and profitable growth.

Now, at this point in my career, I am seeking to transition my experience into a broad-based general management position with a growing and dynamic city government. Thus my interest in your search for a Finance Director and request for a personal interview.

Highlights of my professional career that may be of particular interest to you include the following:

- Active participation, in cooperation with Mayor, City Council and other government officials, in the planning and leadership of large municipal organizations (servicing up to 80,000 residents).

- Expertise in administrative management, operations planning, departmental operations and inter-departmental coordination.

- Development of policies, procedures and standards governing operations, fiscal affairs and technology.

- Strong public speaking and public relations competencies.

- Extensive involvement in high-profile economic and business development programs.

- Leadership of successful public and private funding programs totalling more than $35 million throughout my career.

I am available at your convenience for a personal interview and would be delighted to provide any additional information you may require. Thank you for your time and consideration.

Sincerely,

Jeffery A. Cavanaugh

Enclosure

100

GRADUATING STUDENT

KeyWords, Action Verbs & High-Impact Phrases

To "Nail" Your Cover Letter:

* Course Highlights

* Special Research Projects

* Academic Performance & Standing

* Internships

* Athletic Achievements

* Foreign Language Skills

* PC Skills

* Professional Skills

* Leadership Capabilities

* Volunteerism & Community Service

PAUL E. REINHARDT

119 Old Stable Road
Lynchburg, Virginia 24503
(804) 384-4600

March 28, 1997

Neil Simon
Senior Sales Manager
Nelson Pharmaceuticals
121 Centerpoint Road
Alexandria, VA 23232

Dear Mr. Simon:

First of all, thank you. I appreciate any assistance you can offer in helping me to secure a sales position. My goal is an entry-level professional position with a company offering opportunity, challenge and advancement potential. In return, I offer strong interpersonal relations and communications skills, the ability to independently manage projects from beginning to completion, and a strong desire to excel.

I am currently working as a Sales Associate in a high-volume sales and service organization. I have consistently been ranked as one of the top sales producers and acquired a wealth of experience in order processing and customer service/satisfaction.

An athlete and coach throughout high school and college, I am competitive in nature. I know what I am capable of and confident in my ability. Now I am seeking the opportunity to demonstrate my capabilities in a fast-paced and customer-driven organization.

I would welcome a chance for a personal interview and again thank you for your consideration. Be advised that I am open to relocation and willing to travel as may be necessary.

Sincerely,

Paul E. Reinhardt

Enclosure

RALF BECHER
875 Dawson Road
Orlando, Florida 38917
Phone/Fax (954) 239-0169

August 23, 1997

Director of Engineering
Federal Aviation Administration
1200 Central Avenue, Suite 545
Washington, D.C. 20011

Dear Sir/Madam:

I am just graduating from Embry-Riddle Aeronautical University with a B.S. Degree in Aircraft Engineering Technology. My goal is an entry-level professional position in the aircraft industry where I can combine my academic training, laboratory experience and practical hands-on skills in aircraft engineering, safety and accident investigation.

Most notably, I was selected for a competitive internship with the local FAA office. This was an intensive, on-site program where I acquired excellent experience in ramp inspection, aircraft inspection, flight checks and accident investigation/analysis. It was a great opportunity to translate what I had learned in the classroom into the field.

What distinguishes me from other graduates is not only my technical proficiency, but also my interpersonal relations and cross-cultural communication skills. A native of Switzerland, I have lived and worked in the U.S. for the past five years. As such, my perspective of the airline industry and my knowledge of domestic and international aircraft regulations is strong.

I would welcome the opportunity for a personal interview at your earliest convenience and thank you in advance for your consideration.

Sincerely,

Ralf Becher

Enclosure

JEFFERSON W. YOUNG

Current Address
988-J Greek Hill
Chapel Hill, NC 29213
(919) 549-0625

Permanent Address
121 Shady Acre Drive
 Westminster, VA 23205
(804) 523-0609

April 22, 1997

George Patterson
Managing Partner
Patterson Advertising
1597 Research Triangle Business Park, Suite 200
Raleigh, NC 28797

Dear Mr. Patterson:

Knowing that at this time of year you are probably besieged by college students interested in summer employment opportunities, let me briefly highlight the skills and value I bring to your organization.

- Dedicated commitment to a long and successful career in Public Relations, Communications, Marketing, Promotions & Special Events.

- Excellent public speaking and communication skills, developed through several years of community service, public presentations and customer/guest relations.

- Active athletic career (principally soccer) during which I excelled, winning notable recognition throughout my home state not only for my athletic skill but also my success in team building and group leadership.

- Proven success in prioritizing time and resources to meet project deadlines.

- An energetic, enthusiastic and "people-driven" communication style.

Just completing my junior year at UNC-Chapel Hill, I am interested in a unique summer internship or employment position with hands-on responsibilities in public relations and communications. My performance at UNC-Chapel Hill has been excellent, providing me with strong theoretical and strategic skills. Now I am looking for the opportunity to apply these skills within a professional setting and demonstrate my ability to produce.

I appreciate your time in reviewing my qualifications and look forward to a personal interview. Thank you.

Sincerely,

Jefferson W. Young

Enclosure

JACKIE R. HENDERSON

2540 S. Hacienda Lane
Los Angeles, California 97145

Home (315) 333-2125   School (315) 955-0655   Fax (315) 333-2605

June 16, 1997

Steven P. Dillard
Managing Partner
Dillard Management Consulting, Inc.
100 West Rodeo Drive
Los Angeles, CA 90028

Dear Mr. Dillard:

Please accept this letter as application for a consulting position with Dillard Management Consulting. My resume is enclosed for your review. Highlights of my academic and employment experience include:

* <u>Strong Leadership & Project Management Skills</u>. With extensive experience working on two political campaigns, I have been involved in planning, budgeting, staffing and campaign administration. On campus, I have been an active member and leader of several student organizations, and coordinated a number of marketing, member development and promotional campaigns.

* <u>Excellent Academic Record</u>. Since enrolling at the University of California, I have earned three academic degrees, carried a heavy courseload and maintained a 3.2+ GPA.

* <u>Communications & Public Relations Skills</u>. In each of my positions, I have been responsible for managing communications with customers, constituents and the general public. My skills in interpersonal relations, public speaking and cross-cultural communications are excellent.

* <u>Analytical & Organizational Skills</u>. Both my coursework and my practical employment experience in the financial services and political arenas have allowed me to demonstrate my strengths in data collection and analysis, project organization, administration and reporting.

Now that I am nearing completion of my studies, I am anxious to launch my professional career, and would welcome a personal interview at your earliest convenience. Thank you.

Sincerely,

Jackie R. Henderson

Enclosure

BRIAN SMITH
8398 Desert Highway, Apt. 123
Las Cruces, New Mexico 88012
(505) 334-7555

April 19, 1997

William C. Thomas
President
International Ventures, Inc.
1880 Palmer Avenue
Santa Fe, NM 83535

Dear Mr. Thomas:

I'm looking for a great opportunity!

An upcoming graduate of New Mexico State University with a Bachelor of Business Administration in International Business, I am anxious to begin my professional career. Unlike many of my peers whose only experience is academic, I offer not only strong educational credentials but practical, "hands-on" experience in international business.

Since 1994, I have worked on a part-time basis with an Arizona-based energy company currently expanding throughout the Latin American market. This experience has included evaluating international market opportunities, coordinating communications with international business partners, and assisting in complex international financial transactions. In fact, my role has been quite significant on several occasions as a result of my fluency in both Spanish language and culture.

My primary career goal is international business — either from a finance or sales/marketing orientation. I am seeking challenge and the opportunity to provide my worth and ability to build company value.

I would welcome a personal interview to explore positions with your company and can assure you that my drive, energy and personal goals will enable me to succeed. Thank you.

Sincerely,

Brian Smith

Enclosure

HEALTH CARE

KeyWords, Action Verbs & High-Impact Phrases

To "Nail" Your Cover Letter:

* Revenue & Profit Growth

* New Clinical Services & Provider Networks

* New Revenue Generating Programs & Ventures

* Managed Care Programs

* Technology Implementation

* Capital Project Management

* Risk Management

* Regulatory Affairs & Compliance

* Health Care Policy

* Health Care Service Delivery & Administration

CARL WATSON, M.D.
2649 North Wabash Avenue
Chicago, Illinois 60610

Home (312) 480-9809   **Office (312) 916-4125**

July 9, 1997

James L. Lewis
Executive Recruiter
Lewis & Associates
100 West 49th Street, 15th Floor
New York, NY 10019

Dear Mr. Lewis:

Currently a Director and Executive Committee Member of Memorial West Hospital / Medical School, I am exploring new management opportunities in the emerging health care, managed care, pharmaceutical and biotechnology industries. With more than 15 years of health care management experience, strong clinical qualifications and current attendance in Kellogg's MBA program (expected in 1998), I am seeking the opportunity to combine my skills for a top-level management position.

Beginning my career as a Medical Doctor and Radiologist, I quickly expanded the scope of my responsibility to include a diversity of business management functions — from strategic planning, staffing and budgeting to pioneering programs in technology, quality and performance improvement. In sum, I manage the "business" of medicine.

Notable achievements include recognition by JCAHO for my efforts in quality and regulatory affairs, development of innovative management and professional training programs, publication of research in more than 60 journal articles, and introduction of state-of-the-art information, radiologic and medical systems. I have helped to build a department at Memorial that is not only recognized for its clinical expertise, but just as significantly for its management, financial, technological and quality achievements.

With the addition of my MBA degree, I am now ready to transition my qualifications into the private sector where I can participate in the development, operations and leadership of a successful organization. If you are working with a client company seeking a candidate with my qualifications, I would welcome a personal interview. Please note that I am interested in relocating to New York and that my compensation requirements are flexible. Thank you.

Sincerely,

Carl Watson, M.D.

Enclosure

985 Lakeside Drive
Oshkosh, Michigan 63126
Home (616) 343-8274   Office (616) 343-2804

May 29, 1997

Hospital Search Committee
c/o Grant Cooper & Associates, Inc.
795 Office Parkway, Suite 117
St. Louis, MO 63141-7146

Dear Committee Members:

It is with great interest that I submit my resume for consideration as President & CEO of your client's metropolitan health system. I bring to the position a diversity of experience and strong track record of performance in the strategic planning, development, marketing and management of diversified health care service organizations.

Highlights of my professional career include:

• Fourteen years of top-flight executive management experience in the health care services and products industries.

• Expertise in the start-up of new health care ventures and accelerated growth within existing provider organizations.

• Delivery of strong revenue and profit growth within extremely competitive and volatile health care markets.

• Strong qualifications in community outreach and public affairs, particularly as they pertain to building managed care networks and service organizations.

• Broad-based general management skills in MIS technology, human resource affairs, training, facilities and materials management, general accounting, financial planning and analysis, budgeting, board presentations and other senior-level operating management functions.

• Extensive network of professional, technical, financial and medical contacts throughout the health care community.

My leadership style is direct and decisive, yet I am flexible in responding to the constantly changing demands of my staff, management team, customers and market. I am familiar with most regulations governing health care practice, and have been the driving force behind several financially and operationally successful organizations.

I look forward to speaking with you to further pursue this opportunity. Compensation requirements can be discussed at the time of our interview. Thank you.

Sincerely,

Thomas P. Windsor

Enclosure

PETER C. ROBINSON
28 Granite Street
Houston, TX 55432
(201) 874-6251

June 1, 1997

Oscar Munoz
Executive Director
Imperial Managed Care
19290 Southwest Boulevard
Oklahoma City, OK 59874

Dear Mr. Munoz:

For the past 12 years, I have held a series of increasingly responsible positions within the Health Care industry, gaining extensive experience in virtually all core functions impacting the industry. My particular areas of expertise include Managed Care and Provider Relations with additional strengths in:

* Strategic Planning, Marketing and Business Development
* Health Care Delivery & Service Models
* Supplier/Vendor Relationships & Negotiations
* Revenue-Generating Programs & Services
* Market-Driven Quality & Productivity Improvements
* Regulatory, Legislative and Policy Issues

My greatest strength lies in my ability to identify and capitalize upon market opportunity to drive revenue growth, improve competitive market positioning and enhance the quality of service. Equally significant are my qualifications in organizational leadership, including planning, staffing, training, public relations, communications, advertising and government affairs.

Although currently employed as Director of Marketing for a senior life care community, the opportunities for long-term advancement are quite limited. Further, I desire to return to a more focused health care organization and would welcome the opportunity to interview with Imperial Managed Care.

I look forward to speaking with you at your earliest convenience and appreciate your time in reviewing my qualifications. I'm confident that the strength of my industry experience, combined with my dedication, energy and commitment, will add measurable value to your organization. Thank you.

Sincerely,

Peter C. Robinson

Enclosure

THOMAS F. MENDLESON
15186 Yucca Drive
Peoria, Arizona 85381
(602) 882-7064

March 17, 1997

Joseph M. Parker
Chairman
Kaiser Medical, Inc.
1990 Seaport Avenue
San Francisco, CA 93245

Dear Mr. Parker:

I am writing in response to your advertisement for a President/CEO and have enclosed my resume for your review.

As a member of the senior management team of Medical Care Corporation since 1981, I have been a driving force behind the substantial growth and diversification of the company. Starting with a limited product line and a small specialty market, the president and I have transformed the corporation into a $75 million revenue producer with a diversified consumables and equipment portfolio and nationwide market share. My specific contributions have included:

- Development and leadership of a national sales, marketing, field service and customer support organization (both direct and distributor).

- Identification and negotiation of joint ventures and other strategic partnerships which have increased product offerings, expanded sales capabilities and placed Medical Care in a proactive, high-profile market position.

- Start-up of an autonomous field service organization and independent profit center that now generates over $4 million in annual revenues to the corporation.

- Start-up of a Medical Equipment Division as part of Medical Care's aggressive diversification program. This business now produces over $12 million in revenues on an annual basis.

- Management of annual business planning, market research, product development/evaluation, staffing, budget, administration and other general operating functions.

Although secure in my current position, I am confidentially investigating new professional opportunities. My years at Medical Care have be very rewarding; however I am now seeking new challenges. Please feel free to contact me during the day, in confidence, at (602) 111-1500. I appreciate your consideration and look forward to speaking with you.

Sincerely,

Thomas F. Mendleson

Enclosure

JAY LESTER, M.D.
541-4th Street
New York, New York 10019
(212) 460-3324

February 28, 1997

Adam Washington
Managing Partner
Healthcare Executives Worldwide
1874 Avenue of the Americas, 43rd Floor
New York, NY 11542

Dear Mr. Washington:

I am a well-qualified Health Care / Hospital Administrator with 16 years of professional experience in the development, budgeting, staffing and management of multi-specialty health care programs and services. Highlights of my professional career include:

- Extensive experience in the introduction of quality assurance, utilization review and internal audit programs that have consistently enhanced the delivery of health care services.

- Establishment of health care policy governing large regional health care and managed care networks throughout the U.S., Canada, South America and Europe.

- Implementation of aggressive cost controls that have reduced annual expenditures with no negative impact on the quality of care or care providers.

- Excellent qualifications managing relationships with Boards of Directors, Finance Directors, major donors, regulators and others involved in health care planning and funding.

- Full management responsibility for all general business functions (e.g., budgeting, physician recruitment, staff training, facilities, provider relations, public relations, insurance administration).

I have most recently travelled throughout the jungles of South America, working with local physicians, nurses and health care administrators to facilitate the development of preventive medicine, nutrition and immunization programs. Now that I have returned to the U.S., I am anxious to again assume an administrative assignment with a hospital, clinic or other health care organization, and would welcome a personal interview to discuss potential opportunities. Thank you.

Sincerely,

Jay Lester, M.D.

Enclosure

HOSPITALITY

KeyWords, Action Verbs & High-Impact Phrases

To "Nail" Your Cover Letter:

* Guest Services & Public Relations

* Revenue & Profit Improvement

* Occupancy Increases

* Capital Improvement & Renovation

* Corporate, Association & Group Sales Achievements

* Operating & Labor Cost Reductions

* Quality & Service Awards & Recognition

* Technology Enhancements

* New Property Development & Start-Up

* Amenities Programs

FRANK NELSON, JR.

425 Armadillo Avenue
Rosemont, Texas 78482

Residence   (210) 469-3544
Business/Fax   (210) 469-3545
Pager   (800) 631-9832

February 14, 1997

Paul Kirwin
President - Country Inns & Suites
Country Hospitality Worldwide
Carlson Parkway
P.O. Box 59159
Minneapolis, MN 55459-8203

Dear Mr. Kirwin:

Congratulations! I've been watching the development of your new property in Rosemont, Texas and can tell you that the entire community is looking forward to the grand opening. We've needed a property of this type in Rosemont for several years (as I'm sure your demographics indicated) and I know that the project will be extremely profitable if well led.

I'm a local resident of Rosemont with a wealth of business experience worldwide. Having recently relocated permanently to the area, I would welcome the opportunity to interview with you or a member of your staff for the position of General Manager with the local property. Let me tell you why I am the "perfect" candidate (albeit atypical):

- More than 15 years of general management experience in facilities development and operating management, including planning, budgeting, logistics, purchasing, equipment, materials, technology and large-scale customer service.

- Outstanding communication and people-to-people interaction skills. I am well-known throughout the local market, have extensive contacts throughout both the professional and civic communities, and recently completed a yearlong leadership training course with the City.

- Ability to "get the job done" no matter the circumstance. This was particularly critical throughout my career, often working in environments with stringent deadlines and financial expectations.

- Strong qualifications in personnel training, development and leadership with direct responsibility for hundreds of employees, supervisors and managers, and multi-million dollar budgets.

- In-depth understanding of customer service, customer loyalty and customer retention.

I am available at your convenience for a personal interview and guarantee that the strength of my leadership skills and operating performance will position the Rosemont property for strong and profitable growth.

Sincerely,

Frank Nelson, Jr.

Enclosure

LOUIS M. BACHMAN

8410 Westport Lake Drive
Harrisburg, PA 94108
(863) 466-6608

January 12, 1997

Richard Cavin
President
Host International
1973 Palmer Avenue
Albany, NY 13587

Dear Mr. Cavin:

I am a well-qualified Restaurant/Hospitality Industry Professional with 10 years of top-flight management experience. Beginning as an Operating Unit Manager, I have progressed rapidly through a series of increasingly responsible positions to my current assignment as Area Director for multiple operating locations.

My greatest accomplishment has been the development of the Western Pennsylvania market. Starting with a concept, I built market presence, developed five operating locations and generated over $12 million in annual sales. Previous revenue gains where equally impressive; profit performance the best in the corporation and its 52 operating units.

Just as significant are my strengths in personnel, management development, budgeting, financial management, quality assurance and purchasing. In addition, I have worked cooperatively with the MIS technology team to orchestrate the introduction of leading edge systems to automate our processes and improve our organizational structure.

At this point in my career, I am seeking new professional challenges and opportunities where I can continue to provide strong and decisive leadership, build market presence and improve financial results. If you are seeking such a candidate, I would welcome a personal interview and thank you in advance for your consideration.

Sincerely,

Louis M. Bachman

Enclosure

CALVIN HIGHMAN, CHA
1973 South 2500 East
Salt Lake City, Utah 84108
Email: high@net.com
Phone/Fax: (801) 466-6088

April 4, 1997

Larry Jefferson
Executive Vice President
Royal Caribbean Resorts, Inc.
1293 Ocean View Drive
Boca Raton, FL 33532

Dear Mr. Jefferson:

With more than 20 years experience in the Hospitality Industry, I bring to Royal Caribbean a strong record of management performance and achievement in:

* Increasing revenues and bottom-line profits while reducing annual operating, overhead and payroll costs.
* Introducing top-flight quality, service and member retention programs.
* Managing complex financial analysis, budgeting and reporting functions.
* Driving successful sales, marketing and member development programs.

With excellent communications, interpersonal relations, organizational, project management and leadership qualifications, I guarantee that I can far surpass your goals and objectives in your search for a General Manager.

I appreciate your time in reviewing my qualifications and will follow-up promptly. My recent salary history is $105,000 plus full benefits package and a 20% incentive plan.

Sincerely,

Calvin Highman, CHA

Enclosure

HUMAN RESOURCES

KeyWords, Action Verbs & High-Impact Phrases

To "Nail" Your Cover Letter:

* Organizational Development

* Benefits & Compensation

* Training & Development

* Cost Reduction & Avoidance

* HRIS Technology

* Recruitment & Selection

* Succession Planning

* Workforce Integration

* Corporate Culture Change

* Performance Improvement

SAMUEL P. REIDER

7837 S.E. Williams Street
Madison, Wisconsin 82040

Home   (602) 232-4015
Office   (602) 452-2520

May 19, 1997

George B. Schmidt
President
Industrial Manufacturing, Inc.
199 Mississippi Avenue
St. Louis, MO 60545

Dear Mr. Schmidt:

Human Resources is no longer the traditional personnel function and successful managers have recognized this change. Over the past decade as "corporate America" has redefined itself, human resources has become an increasingly vital component in revenue and profit improvement. We have all come to value the strength and potential of our workforce and its influence over our success.

To meet those challenges, I have created HR organizations that are innovative, results-driven and tied directly to bottom-line performance. These programs have ranged from specific business reengineering initiatives to corporate-wide recruitment, staffing and leadership development programs. In turn, financial results have improved and stability has been returned.

Please also note that I have extremely strong generalist qualifications in all core HR functions with particular strengths in labor negotiations and employee relations. Major projects have included benefits and compensation design, succession plans, EH&S program management, quality training and complete workforce realignment programs.

My goal is a senior-level HR executive assignment with a company in need of strong and decisive organizational leadership. After you've reviewed my resume, I would welcome a personal interview and look forward to meeting with you.

Sincerely,

Samuel P. Reider

Enclosure

ELIZABETH LIVINGSTON
13792 S.E. 78th Place
Mercer Island, Washington 98042
Home (206) 401-3525

June 23, 1997

Robert Moser
Executive Vice President
Talbot, Inc.
3000 West Evergreen, Suite 223
Portland, OR 55323

Dear Mr. Moser:

In 1989 I was recruited as the first-ever Director of Human Resources for a 130-year-old organization. Starting with a workforce of 60 employees and virtually no formal HR policies, I built a top-flight HR organization, introduced innovative training and performance management programs, negotiated self-funded benefit programs and led the organization through a period of rapid growth to more than 250 employees at three operating locations.

In early 1996, I accepted the opportunity to spearhead the reorganization of the complete HR and organizational development function following the merger of two of Canada's most respected and innovative investment firms to form Allied Smith, Inc. To date, I have created a cohesive operating infrastructure and recruited 30+ senior management and professionals to support Allied's market launch throughout the U.S.

These experiences have been tremendous and afforded me the opportunity to create innovative HR and employee relations programs that have consistently strengthened our operating performance. However, due to unforeseen changes within the Allied organization, I am now exploring new professional opportunities where I can continue to provide strong and decisive HR leadership. Thus my interest in Talbot and request for a personal interview.

Please note that my academic credentials include an MBA in Human Resources and an MS in Industrial Relations.

I appreciate your consideration and will follow-up next week to arrange a time for a personal interview. Thank you.

Sincerely,

Elizabeth Livingston

Enclosure

EUGENE S. THOMPSON, CCP

P.O. Box 156
Washington, D.C 21056
Email: est@aol.com

Home (202) 624-1465
Office (202) 783-2210
Fax   (202) 783-3322

August 18, 1997

Jeffry Lawrence
President
Inacomp Technology Manufacturing
122 Kroger Drive
Spokane, WA 99056

Dear Mr. Lawrence:

Strong human resources leadership can have a tremendous impact on corporate and organizational value. By building an effective HR infrastructure, providing strategic HR leadership, and controlling escalating compensation and benefit costs, you can immediately improve the financial performance, productivity and viability of your organization.

This is the value I deliver.

An accomplished HR executive with strong qualifications in all core generalist functions, I have been instrumental in strengthening performance through my efforts in:

- Union, Management & Labor Relations
- Domestic & International Staffing
- Employee Training & Development
- Safety Management & Control
- Benefits & Compensation Design

- HRIS Technology
- Quality & Productivity
- Employee Relations
- Regulatory Compliance
- Employee Law & Litigation

I am a proactive business manager, credited with the development of innovative productivity, efficiency, quality and performance management programs with strong bottom-line results. Further, my ability to build cooperation — between union and non-union personnel — between employees and operating management teams — between field and headquarters organizations — has been critical to our overall performance.

Although secure in my current position, I am confidentially exploring new professional challenges and opportunities. Thus my interest in discussing your search for a Corporate Human Resources Director.

I appreciate your consideration and look forward to speaking with you in the next few days.

Sincerely,

Eugene S. Thompson, CCP

Enclosure

120

NELSON M. BRIGHTSEN

176 Renaissance Circle
El Paso, Texas 79936-7176

Voice Mail (915) 388-7853 x250   Residence (915) 857-6392

March 3, 1997

William Shepheard
Chairman of the Board
Emergency Air Conditioning Company
P.O. Box 2496
Norfolk, VA 23501-2496

Dear Mr. Shepheard:

Managing human resource performance issues within large and complex industrial manufacturing organizations is a challenge! There are, of course, all the "typical" HR generalist functions found in any company. But within our industry, there is so much more — union issues, union avoidance issues, safety and quality issues, continuous process improvement and productivity/performance issues.

I have positively met all of these challenges, building HR organizations responsive to both management and worker needs. By facilitating cooperation and commitment to common goals, we have avoided potentially difficult situations and achieved some of the highest productivity ratings in the industry.

Just as critical are my contributions to the bottom-line:

- Currently nearing completion of QS-9000 quality certification process for GAP Systems.
- $4 million in operating cost savings for Signal Resources.
- $1.3 million contribution to cash flow for a multi-site service organization.
- Operating unit turnaround from $10 million loss to $10 million profit.

Currently, and confidentially, I am exploring new career challenges and opportunities in an effort to return to the Mid-Atlantic region. As such, I would welcome a personal interview at your convenience. Thank you.

Sincerely,

Nelson M. Brightsen

Enclosure

FRANCES HACKETT

2305 South Pittsburg Street
Stilwell, Kansas 66762

Residence   (316) 231-1690
Office   (417) 781-3645

May 23, 1997

William Jones
President
Monsanto Corporation
298 West River Road
St. Louis, MO 65898

Dear Mr. Jones:

I am a well-qualified Training & Development Executive with more than 15 years' experience in program design and delivery. My expertise lies in my ability to identify organizational needs and develop training programs responsive to all levels of personnel throughout an organization. Just as significant are my contributions to improved business performance, productivity, quality and profitability.

Highlights of my career include:

- Participated in the start-up of new professional training organization to enhance the business, technical, legal, IS and professional skills of personnel throughout Smith Rand.

- Development and delivery of more than 57,000 student hours of training and incentive programs that generated solid operating and cost contributions for Signal Enterprises.

- Introduction of cross-functional training programs into Clement's manufacturing organization and capture of over $1.1 million in cost savings.

I am a strong business leader and talented instructor with the ability to impact positive change and improvement. My goal is a senior-level training and development management position with a company seeking strong, decisive and dedicated leadership.

I look forward to meeting with you and thank you in advance for your consideration.

Sincerely,

Frances Hackett

Enclosure

122

WOODROW T. HOOVER

2877 Windsong Drive
Eden, New York 14067

Phone (716) 532-3939   **Fax (716) 997-2451**

September 17, 1997

Charles Hoffman
President
Brixton, Inc.
983 Stout Avenue
Lutherville, MD 21093

Dear Mr. Hoffman:

Building value is my expertise. As a driving force behind the development of leading edge training, organization development and management development programs for several large corporations, I have consistently impacted the quality, productivity, efficiency and cost performance of operations. My strength lies in my ability to evaluate organizational needs and develop responsive training programs to exploit core competencies and enhance the participation of each and every employee in the long-term growth of the organization.

As you will note, my career has spanned a diversity of industries — from newspaper publishing to international construction and engineering. Despite the environment, I have been consistently successful in improving results through my efforts in building and strengthening the human resources function.

Most significant are my efforts in partnering HR with operations, stressing to management the critical impact of its employees upon the long-term performance of their business units. In turn, I positioned myself as a key advisor and advocate to top management, translating their objectives into actionable performance plans.

After a strong and performance-driven career with The Eden Register, I unfortunately was part of the company's most recent downsizing initiative. Since that date, I have begun to consult with local corporations on a diversity of training and OD initiatives. However, my goal is another top-level position where I can continue to drive organizational growth and performance improvement. Thus my interest in Brixton, Inc. and request for a personal interview.

Sincerely,

Woodrow T. Hoover

Enclosure

STEVEN T. GIBRALTAR
2877 Wood Spirit
Eden, New York 14057
(716) 992-3879

October 4, 1997

John Billings
President
Billings Manufacturing, Inc.
One Dove Plaza
Orland Park, IL 60462

Dear Mr. Billings:

As markets, products and industries become increasingly competitive, companies are faced with unprecedented financial and operating challenges. To achieve and maintain market dominance, there are certain initiatives a firm can undertake to ensure a competitive advantage. One of those initiatives is to build a strong human resource function, putting in place the personnel and corporate culture essential to further growth and profitability.

As a Senior HR Executive, I have met those challenges and been a key contributor to the sustained growth and financial gain of several organizations. Most notably:

- <u>Industrial Metals Corporation.</u> Member of executive team orchestrating the successful turnaround of the corporation with 143% improvement in revenues and profitability.

- <u>Smithfield Bank</u>. Reengineered 2200-employee workforce and delivered a 46% reduction in annual staffing costs.

- <u>P.J. Arnold Company</u>. Captured $300,000+ in annual benefit cost savings.

The scope of my experience spans the entire HR function — recruitment, staffing, benefits, HRIS, employee relations, training and development, succession planning and performance/productivity improvement. Unlike many of my peers, I have equally strong experience in purchasing, quality, contracts, government relations, fleet management and corporate administration. It is the sum of these that has provided me with the qualifications to initiate the action and deliver the results so critical to the long-term performance of each organization.

Now, at this point in my career, I am seeking a senior-level HR and administrative management position where I can continue to drive forward critical performance improvement, organizational development and change management initiatives. I look forward to speaking with you to pursue opportunities with Billings Manufacturing and appreciate your consideration. Thank you.

Sincerely,

Steven T. Gilbraltar

Enclosure

124

KEITH ROTHSAY, SPHR
9021 North Haledon
Newark, New Jersey 07508
(201) 474-3601

October 21, 1997

Thomas Malcolm
President
Horace Industrial
1232 Cedar Street
Memphis, TN 44551

Dear Mr. Malcolm:

Bringing innovative and decisive human resources leadership has been the foundation for my success through-out the past 10+ years. As the Vice President/Director of Human Resources for the $100 million Crystal Metal Services Company, I have pioneered HR, employee relations and labor relations programs that have been the catalyst for tremendous organizational growth and financial gain. Most notably:

* Negotiated over $500,000 in labor cost savings.
* Reengineered core business processes and saved over $1.2 million in workers' compensation, benefit, administration and MIS costs.
* Led a successful workforce reduction initiative with no lawsuits or arbitration.
* Introduced participative management, quality management, leadership training and other performance-driven initiatives.

Complementing my extensive qualifications in HR management are strong skills in Accounting, Administration, Purchasing, Strategic Business Planning and MIS. Working in cooperation with top-level operating and management teams, I have provided the organizational direction and leadership critical to meeting production, quality, cost and revenue objectives.

After a long and successful career with Crystal, the company has undergone a massive reorganization following its recent acquisition. Currently, I am facilitating the workforce reengineering process while continuing to pursue new professional opportunities. My goal is a senior-level HR management position with a high-growth organization and, as such, I would welcome a personal interview to explore such positions with your organization. Thank you.

Sincerely,

Keith Rothsay, SPHR

Enclosure

AMANDA P. CHURCHILL
293 Aspen Drive
Littleton, Colorado 82508
(301) 427-5640

September 4, 1997

Wilson Price
President/CEO
Lancaric International
P.O. Box 1935
Newport, RI 23532-1935

Dear Mr. Price:

Building organizational value is my expertise. As the Senior Human Resources Executive for a high-growth manufacturing/marketing organization, I have supported the company's growth from a small, US-based operation into a world class global corporation with a talented, production-driven and stable workforce.

The challenges of the position have been enormous. Starting with a paper-only HR function and a staff of personnel clerks, today we are a fully automated organization providing HR policy, programs and leadership for 1400 employees in 12 countries worldwide. Through this transition, I have provided the strategic and tactical action to develop strong benefit, compensation, employee relations, union avoidance, recruitment and training programs.

Please also note that I have particularly strong skills in executive recruitment and development for both U.S. and international operations. Throughout my career, I have been the catalyst for these programs across diverse industries, markets and geographies.

My employer, Mintz Manufacturing, is currently downsizing and reengineering its operations worldwide. As such, I am exploring new professional opportunities with organizations seeking strong, decisive and market-driven HR leadership. I look forward to interviewing for the position of Human Resources Director and would expect compensation in the range of $125,000 to $150,000 annually. Thank you.

Sincerely,

Amanda P. Churchill

Enclosure

BRUCE MELBOURNE, JR.
1462 Gator Swamp Drive
Saratoga Springs, Florida 39240
(753) 223-8695

January 13, 1997

Mark Garrison
President
Johnson Wire & Cable, Inc.
1923 Portsmouth Causeway
Dearborn, OH 76532

Dear Mr. Garrison:

Are you in need of strong and decisive human resources leadership? If so, please consider the following highlights of my professional career:

- More than 10 years' senior-level experience as an HR Generalist providing HR planning and leadership worldwide.

- Expert qualifications in training and development with particular emphasis on creating training programs responsive to changing organizational needs and a large, multinational workforce.

- Implementation of HRIS technology and applications to improve information flow, availability and use in long-range strategic planning and development initiatives.

- Strong qualifications in employee relations, grievances and regulatory affairs.

- Ability to build confidence and trust between employees and management, creating environments that support and reward individual accomplishment and contribution to the "larger whole".

Most significantly, I have positioned myself and my HR organizations as an ally to senior management, working to build top-producing, top-performing workforces able to meet operating challenges. My leadership and guidance to these top executives has been one of the most critical contributors to our gains in performance, quality and productivity.

My goal is a senior-level HR position with an organization seeking talent, drive, enthusiasm and leadership expertise. Thus my interest in meeting with you to explore such opportunities with Johnson Wire & Cable, Inc. Thank you.

Sincerely,

Bruce Melbourne, Jr.

Enclosure

INSURANCE

KeyWords, Action Verbs & High-Impact Phrases

To "Nail" Your Cover Letter:

* Agency Operations

* Risk Management

* Asset Management & Loss Control

* Business Reorganization & Operations Improvement

* Regulatory Reporting & Compliance

* Premium Processing & Billing Operations

* Key Account Wins & Revenue Performance

* Home Office Operations

* Regional & National Sales Management

* Policy & Claims Administration

MICHAEL SEGAL
5901 Flower Meadows
Chevy Chase, Maryland 22093

Phone (301) 821-7510

Office (301) 583-7092

June 12, 1997

David Williams
Chairman & CEO
State Farm Insurance
935 North Michigan Avenue
Chicago, IL 60611

Dear Mr. Williams:

Designing creative insurance coverages and risk management programs for construction wrap-ups, celebrity tours, motion picture productions and other high-profile projects is my expertise.

Working worldwide (emphasis in the U.S., Asia, Australia and Middle East), I have guided presidents, CEOs and other top-flight executives through the complex insurance cycle to ensure that their assets are protected, their exposures limited and their liabilities greatly diminished. It is just this expertise I bring to you and to State Farm.

Complementing my consummate knowledge of the insurance industry and unique insurance coverages, I also bring a unprecedented record of achievement in structuring and negotiating sensitive contractual agreements — for insurance, mergers, acquisitions, joint ventures and other cooperative alliances. Whether working as a CEO, Chairman, Vice President or COO, I have provided the strategic and tactical leadership critical to building agency volumes worldwide.

Now, at this juncture in my career, I am seeking new senior-level management opportunities with an insurance brokerage that prides itself on the quality, strength and performance of its products and services. With more than 20 years of industry experience, I have come to know the major players worldwide. Repeatedly, State Farm has been brought to my attention — recognized for not only the quality of its insurance programs, but the strength and determination of your leadership.

I now look to you for new career opportunities where I can continue to provide decisive leadership under your direction, and look forward to what I anticipate will be the first of many positive communications. Thank you.

Sincerely,

Michael Segal

Enclosure

129

THOMAS KEELER
349 Indian Trail Road
Cincinnati, Ohio 45632
(845) 533-6532

November 21, 1997

James Williams
President & CEO
Brennan Insurance, Inc.
9348 River Valley Road
Indianapolis, IN 43562

Dear Mr. Williams:

With 20 years' experience in the Insurance Industry, I bring to your organization a wealth of qualifications in the strategic planning, development and profitable leadership of both agency and Home Office operations. My expertise lies in my ability to identify and capitalize upon market opportunities to increase premium growth, accelerate commission income and outperform competition. Most notably, I:

* Delivered a 32% increase in P&C production for Farm Bureau.

* Led the successful reorganization of Allied's Midwestern Region, driving an 84.% increase in annual premium volume.

* Built Home Life Insurance from start-up to $700,000 in first year revenues.

These achievements are indicative of the quality and caliber of my entire professional career. Whether challenged to launch a new insurance venture, accelerate growth within existing agency operations or lead the successful turnaround of a dormant organization, I have consistently delivered results.

Not only have my numbers been strong, I have repeatedly demonstrated strong management and leadership qualifications and developed other industry professionals now recognized as top producers and managers in their own right. My resume details some of my most significant commendations.

Now, at this point in my career, I am seeking new professional challenges and opportunities where I can continue to provide strong, decisive and market-driven leadership. Thus my interest in your organization and request for a personal interview.

Thank you.

Sincerely,

Thomas Keeler

Enclosure

130

GEORGE N. WILSON
Avenida del Sol
Edificio 21, Apt. 2B
Mexico City, Mexico
552-87-333-3346

February 10, 1997

Scott Weitzman
Managing Partner
Weitzman Insurance
459 Main Street, Suite 12
Stamford, CT 10635

Dear Mr. Weitzman:

I am currently in the process of relocating to the U.S. and am writing to express my interest in professional sales opportunities with Weitzman Insurance. Highlights of my professional career include:

* Fast-track promotion throughout six-year career in the Insurance industry, from field producer to supervisor to regional manager.

* Record of top-level production as both sales producer and sales manager with consistent over-quota performance in revenue growth, profit growth and expense control.

* Management responsibility for a 150-agent regional sales network.

* Strong communication, leadership, negotiation and motivational skills.

I am particularly successful in identifying market opportunities and creating the appropriate sales and business development plans to accelerate growth, outperform competition and build long-term revenues. I am decisive in my actions, yet flexible in response to constantly changing market demands.

My goal is to transition my skills into a U.S. based insurance company where I can continue to drive revenue growth and build a strong customer base. As such, I would welcome the opportunity to speak with you at your earliest convenience, and thank you in advance for your consideration.

Sincerely,

George N. Wilson

Enclosure

INTERNATIONAL MARKETING
&
BUSINESS DEVELOPMENT

KeyWords, Action Verbs & High-Impact Phrases

To "Nail" Your Cover Letter:

* Country & Region Management

* Sales & Profit Growth

* Market Share Improvements

* Public & Private Partnerships

* Mergers & Acquisitions

* Joint Ventures

* Customer Partnerships & Alliances

* Cross-Cultural Communications & Workforce Management

* New Business Development

* Key Account Wins

IVAN VAN DYKE

#1543 Provincial Villa
35 Dongyong Ku Street
100027 Beijing, PRC
Phone/FAX 86-10-6833227

June 1, 1997

Frank Carson
Executive Vice President - Asia
Merrill Lynch Investments Worldwide
1900 Carlyle Avenue, Suite 259
Los Angeles, CA 98633

Dear Mr. Carson:

I am currently the General Sales & Business Manager for Crosby's operation in Beijing. Within less than two years, we have increased billings by 150%+ and built a strong and high-profile reputation. Further, we have strengthened the market positioning of each of our clients — Bausch & Lomb, Coca-Cola, Wools of New Zealand and numerous others.

Living and working in the Far East for the past five years, I have developed an extensive network of contacts with government, corporate and industrial business leaders throughout the region. This is the value I bring to Merrill Lynch. I know the people, the culture, the economy and the market. Only when you have lived in the region for a period of time can you begin to become part of that culture and a respected business professional within the local marketplace.

My goal is a senior-level management position where I can direct sales, marketing, operations, customer service, administration, human resources and finance of an organization within the Far East — quite similar to the responsibilities I manage today. However, my goal is to affiliate with an organization offering opportunities for professional growth, management and leadership.

Please note that I am conversational in five different languages and have tremendous cross-cultural business experience.

I look forward to speaking with you to pursue opportunities with Merrill Lynch.

Sincerely,

Ivan Van Dyke

Enclosure

133

REBECCA KENDRICK
1298 Mi Suk Dong, Songdo Yu
Seoul, Korea
Phone/FAX 663-52-658027

October 14, 1997

Philip Schatzer
President
Asia Investment Ventures
394 45th Street South
New York, NY 10010

Dear Mr. Schatzer:

Building market value and driving revenue is what I do best. With eight years of field sales and marketing management responsibility throughout Europe and the Far East, I bring to your organization a strong record of performance:

* Currently, as General Manager for Bertram's Korean operation, I built and led the team that grew billings by 146% in the first year.

* As International Sales Manager with CPD, I spearheaded the start-up of a new marketing organization to capture emerging opportunities throughout the Pacific Rim.

* During my early sales and operating management career in Europe, I coordinated service, logistics and administration for key customer accounts worldwide.

Equally notable are my strengths in personnel recruitment, training and development. Working with a multinational workforce is always a challenge that requires decisive leadership, a focused commitment to training and top-flight cross-cultural communication skills.

My goal is a senior-level sales and marketing management position with a company seeking strong expansion throughout international markets. As such, my interest in meeting with you to explore such opportunities with Asia Investment. Thank you.

Sincerely,

Rebecca Kendrick

Enclosure

BRADLEY INGLE

394 Memorial Avenue
Nashua, New Hampshire 53803
Phone / Fax (601) 884-9315

October 9, 1997

Stewart Needleson
President - International Operations
Colgate-Palmolive
1222 Colgate Avenue
Larchmont, New York 65354

Dear Mr. Needleson:

I've lived and worked all over the world — from Latin America to Africa, from the Middle East to the Pacific Rim. My challenge in each region has been to build new business and capture emerging revenue opportunities. And, I have succeeded:

- Most recently, I delivered 75% growth in international sales revenues within one year for Snyder Cosmetics.

- As General Manager of Lewis-Brown's Latin American organization, I increased sales 295%, improved operating profit 36% and brought market share to 89%.

- In Chile, I improved sales 175% and increased profits 28% for Cyprus Drug.

- As Managing Director / Marketing & Sales Director for Prince Products, I launched the start-up of operations in Egypt, increased revenues in Greece from $6 million to $25 million and grew French sales by more than $140 million.

These achievements reflect the core of my career — build new markets, negotiate new partnerships, and drive long-term revenue and profit growth. Just as notable are my strengths in general management, team building and leadership, manufacturing operations and finance/asset management. I am direct and decisive in my management style, yet flexible in responding to the constantly changing demands of markets worldwide.

My goal is a senior-level marketing, business development or general management position either in the U.S. or abroad, and I would welcome the opportunity to explore such positions with Colgate-Palmolive. Thank you.

Sincerely,

Bradley Ingle

Enclosure

135

JOHN ERICKSON
2102 Radnor Circle
Denver, Colorado 30003
(303) 333-3003

January 6, 1997

Patrick Stevenson
President
DMG International
198 Webster Avenue, Suite 12
Forest Lake, MN 55025

Dear Mr. Stevenson:

Building international market value is my expertise. Whether challenged to create initial market presence for an emerging equipment company or accelerate revenues within established international markets, I have consistently delivered strong and sustainable financial gains:

- Built $4.2 million dealer network in China.
- Transitioned Australian dealer network from loss to profitability with $2.7 million sales increase in one year.
- Increased Pac Rim sales 59% within first year.
- Negotiated and closed $2.6 million competitive contract in Saudi Arabia.

These achievements are indicative of the quality and caliber of my entire professional career — identify and capture emerging market opportunities and drive long-term revenue growth. Most critical have been my successes in building cooperative business relationships across diverse nationalities and cultures.

Equally significant to note is my extensive background in heavy construction and industrial equipment. With 19 years experience in the industry, I know the products, the competition and the markets. In addition, I bring to your organization strong general management, financial, staffing and technology skills.

I would welcome the opportunity for a personal interview and appreciate your time in reviewing my qualifications. Thank you.

Sincerely,

John Erickson

Enclosure

WILLIAM FREEMAN
282 Cherry Tree Court
Overland Park, Kansas 65323
(602) 547-8954

March 7, 1997

Brian Masterson
Managing Partner
Masterson Global Ventures, Inc.
2349 Cross Country Trail
Denver, CO 58763

Dear Mr. Masterson:

I am a well-qualified International Business Development, Sales & Marketing Executive with 19 years' experience in the Advanced Technology Industry. Currently I am exploring new professional opportunities with a company seeking strong and decisive international leadership.

My qualifications include:

- Excellent cross-cultural communications and business development skills.
- Management responsibility for both direct and dealer/distributor sales networks.
- Personal selling and management responsibility for key multinational accounts.
- Success in both high-growth and "restart" international markets.
- Strong technical product knowledge.
- Excellent training and leadership skills.

If you are working with a client company seeking a candidate with my qualifications, I would welcome the opportunity to speak with you. Be advised that I am open to relocation worldwide and that my salary requirements are $150,000+. Thank you.

Sincerely,

William Freeman

Enclosure

298 Piney Forest
Summerville, South Carolina 75332

Phone: (802) 339-3980   Fax: (802) 339-4276

August 23, 1997

James Van Atta
President
Birch Machinery Company
1200 Executive Suites, Room 123
Detroit, MI 43565

Dear Mr. Van Atta:

When I joined Baxter Industries in 1992, I was challenged to launch the start-up of their first-ever Mexican operations. Over the next three years, I spearheaded an aggressive market research initiative, authored business and marketing plans, recruited local sales and service talent, established distribution channels, and firmly positioned the corporation for long-term market growth.

Previously in my career, I consulted with several U.S. corporations seeking to enter not only the Latin American markets, but also the U.S. and Asia. To each company, I provided strong support in business development, marketing, cross-cultural communications and project management.

With an MBA (emphasis in International Business) and several years of strong international management experience, I bring to Birch Machinery Company the ability to build opportunity and capture new revenues. My goal is to secure a position where I can utilize the strength of my international exposure while continuing to develop my general management and sales/marketing management qualifications.

I would welcome the opportunity to explore positions within your organization and appreciate your time in reviewing my qualifications. Please note that in addition to the above-referenced experience, I also have strong skills in engineering and technology.

Thank you. I look forward to speaking with you.

Sincerely,

Benjamin J. Ross

Enclosure

HENRY AARONSON
9384 Blue Jay Way
Portland, Maine 75233

Home (207) 829-9639   Office (207) 594-1700

May 2, 1997

Colin Byrd
Hatha International
1200 Bakersfield Avenue
Des Moines, IA 51531

Dear Mr. Byrd:

Employed with R.T.C.C., Inc. for the past nine years, I have been instrumental in the development, global market expansion and profitability of this international trade and import/export corporation (operations in Israel, The Netherlands, Russia and the U.S.). My role has been to identify and develop international trade opportunities to introduce new products into emerging markets and build new revenue streams. As you review my resume you will note that the value I have brought to the organization can be measured by significant gains in revenue, volume and market presence.

Inherent in my responsibilities been the negotiation of complex strategic alliances between multinational business partners. My strengths in building profitable ventures and facilitating cooperation among diverse business cultures has been the foundation for the company's success and continued expansion.

Most notable has been my innovative efforts in barter trade management, bringing together vastly different business partners and facilitating transactions to transfer products between cultures, countries and continents. My success in developing and negotiating these partnerships is notable.

In addition to my international trade responsibilities, I have also developed and profitably managed joint venture manufacturing and production operations worldwide to supplement our trade programs and expand our product portfolio. Further, I have built distribution networks to accelerate global market expansion.

Now, at this point in my career, I am seeking new professional challenges and opportunities in international trade and import/export. Thus my interest in Hatha International and request for a personal interview. Thank you.

Sincerely,

Henry Aaronson

Enclosure

LAW

KeyWords, Action Verbs & High-Impact Phrases

To "Nail" Your Cover Letter:

* Corporate Legal Affairs & Policy

* Litigation & Trial Wins

* Regulatory Compliance

* Legislative Advocacy & Lobbying

* Intellectual Property

* Financial & Contract Transactions

* Budgeting & Cost Reduction

* Joint Ventures, Alliances & Partnerships

* IPOs & Secondary Offerings

* New Venture Formation

FREDERICK HAMILTON, ESQ.

2063 Lakeside Drive   Home (847) 664-3520
Glenview, Illinois 60025   Office (847) 390-3244

February 12, 1997

Carey Thurman
President
InterLease, Inc.
1298 South Bend
Summit, New Jersey 07901

Dear Mr. Thurman:

As Corporate Counsel / General Counsel for several start-up and high-growth corporations, I have provided critical legal, technical, financial, "deal making" and operating expertise. My contributions have been instrumental in accelerating market launch, expansion and revenue growth. Most notably, I:

- Delivered a 40% reduction in overhead costs through legal departmental reengineering and process improvement initiatives.

- Provided comprehensive legal guidance in the formation and initial operating start-up of Baxterman Leasing, a venture launched to capitalize upon emerging opportunities within the technology leasing market.

- Revitalized CSR's marketing and business development effort and negotiated/closed over $50 million in new leasing transactions.

- Spearheaded the start-up of BCI Corporation, structured all legal agreements and transactions, and personally negotiated over $20 million in equity sales within the first two years.

The role of corporate counsel has often been viewed as a support function with its primary focus in planning, corporate development, transactions management and litigation. My career includes responsibility for all of these functions, but has expanded to include active participation in the daily operations, marketing and financial success of each organization. It is this diversity of experience and track record of achievement that positions me as a valuable asset to any financial services organization.

I would welcome the opportunity to speak with you regarding your current executive staffing and corporate counsel needs. You will find that my ability to relate the legal functions to daily operations is of significant operating and financial value. Thank you.

Sincerely,

Frederick Hamilton, Esq.

Enclosure

141

DOUGLAS McMILLAN, ESQ.
3412 Landon Street
Rochester, New York 12315
(716) 471-8783

February 12, 1997

Michael K. Brooks
President
Piedmont Investments, Inc.
1110 Highland Avenue, Suite 393
Sunnyvale, CO 65323

Dear Mr. Brooks:

I am a well-qualified and accomplished Corporate Counsel / General Counsel with 12 years' experience in the Financial Services Industry. The scope of my career has included start-up ventures, high-growth corporations and complex turnaround organizations. To each, I have delivered strong and sustainable operating, revenue and earnings gains.

Highlights of my career that may be of particular interest to you include:

- Extensive qualifications in bankruptcy, corporate claims and litigation management.
- Management of complex due diligence reviews for successful U.K.-based IPO.
- Favorable negotiation of over $2 million in credit workouts and settlements.
- Structure and negotiation of $90+ million in bridge and permanent financing.
- Broad-based experience in employment law and regulatory affairs.
- Expertise in large-dollar real estate and capital leasing transactions.

My greatest strengths lie in my ability to identify and capitalize upon opportunities to build volume, reduce liabilities and improve financial returns. I have excellent presentation and negotiation skills, and have personally managed relationships with institutional and private investors, business partners, large corporate customers and others. My role as corporate counsel has not been "behind the scenes," but rather as an active and visible member of senior-level executive teams.

I would welcome the opportunity to meet with you to explore opportunities with either your investment group and/or one of your portfolio companies. Thank you.

Sincerely,

Douglas McMillan, Esq.

Enclosure

ANDREW P. DONNELLY

2063 Leesville Drive
Fairfield, Illinois 60252

Home (708) 657-7640
Office (708) 374-2904

June 10, 1997

Calvin Powell
President
Tambasco, Inc.
200 Glenview Avenue
St. Paul, MN 55784

Dear Mr. Powell:

With more than 15 years' experience in Corporate Law, I bring to your organization extensive qualifications in:

- International Law — spanning 131 countries worldwide and involving virtually every type of legal transaction.

- Financial Transactions — structuring, negotiating and administering sophisticated, cross-border financial transactions involving multiple parties and millions of dollars in funds.

- Commercial Transactions — negotiating complex business transactions, contracts, licensee and distributor agreements, mergers, acquisitions and divestitures.

Through strong leadership of worldwide legal affairs, I have been instrumental in the tremendous growth and worldwide diversification of Wallace International, spearheading international growth, structuring "first-ever" legal transactions, and providing the foundation for both strong revenue growth and operating cost reductions.

Now, at this juncture in my career, I am seeking new professional opportunities where I can continue to lead a corporate legal function and guide a top-flight executive management team. If you are seeking a candidate with such qualifications, I would welcome a personal interview and thank you in advance for your time and consideration.

Sincerely,

Andrew P. Donnelly

Enclosure

JENNIFER YEARWOOD, ESQ.
8751 Ravine Road
Fayetteville, North Carolina 27066
(919) 637-0815

March 11, 1997

George Lutz
President
Prudential Healthcare
1908 Woodland Avenue
Salem, MA 04453

Dear Mr. Lutz:

As Corporate Counsel / General Counsel for several start-up and high-growth corporations, I have provided critical legal, technical, financial, "deal making" and operating expertise. Currently, as Counsel for an emerging HMO in North Carolina, my challenges have included:

* Development of improved contract strategies and negotiating positions.
* Management of complex due diligence reviews for proposed joint ventures and mergers.
* Implementation of PC technology to automate legal affairs and documentation.
* Review/analysis of complex legislative initiatives impacting the HMO's operations.

Prior to joining the HMO, I progressed rapidly through my earlier corporate counsel positions, working in cooperation with senior operating management of several prestigious corporations. Achievements were notable and included:

* Delivered a 40% reduction in overhead costs through internal reengineering and process improvement.
* Directed legal formation and operations start-up of new technology venture.
* Revitalized one organization's marketing programs and negotiated/closed $50+ million in leasing transactions.
* Spearheaded start-up of new corporation and negotiated $20+ million in equity sales.

My role as Corporate Counsel has transcended all core business functions within each organization. In addition to managing planning, corporate development, transactions and litigation, I have functioned as a participating partner in the operations, marketing and financial success of each organization.

My goal is an in-house Corporate Counsel position with an emerging health care provider organization in need of strong, decisive and proactive leadership. As such, my interest is in meeting with you to explore such opportunities with Prudential Healthcare. I appreciate your consideration and look forward to speaking with you. Thank you.

Sincerely,

Jennifer Yearwood, Esq.

Enclosure

WALTER J. CALDWELL
5 West Princeton Circle
Staten Island, New York 14203
(718) 473-8840

February 3, 1997

Addison Ratcliff
Managing Partner
Brixton, Maddox & Ratcliff
1010 Madison Avenue, Suite 103
New York, NY 11001

Dear Mr. Ratcliff:

I am currently employed as a Senior Associate Attorney in the Real Estate Practice of Frank & Lester. With the firm for the past seven years, I have been built a successful and profitable practice area, based largely upon my strength and expertise in real estate law.

As you review my qualifications, you will note that I have successfully combined the legal functions of the practice with the equally critical responsibilities of client management and representation. My position is highly visible, requiring constant interaction not only with my clients, but with their business partners, financial advisors, investors and tenants.

Throughout my career, I have managed virtually all "routine" real estate functions in combination with a number of sophisticated and contractually-complex transactions. These projects have required innovation in deal structuring and negotiation, and often necessitated exhaustive legal reviews and documentation.

My goal is to continue to practice real estate law. However, I am confidentially exploring opportunities with other firms and would welcome an interview at your convenience. Thank you.

Sincerely,

Walter J. Caldwell

Enclosure

LOGISTICS

KeyWords, Action Verbs & High-Impact Phrases

To "Nail" Your Cover Letter:

* Distribution & Warehousing Operations

* Integrated Logistics Management

* Productivity & Quality Improvements

* Cost Reduction & Avoidance

* Distribution Channel Development

* Transportation & Fleet Management

* Materials & Resource Management

* Team Building & Leadership

* Process Redesign & Automation

* Order Entry & Fulfillment

ALLEN C. BURNS

104 Oakdale Court
Springfield, Massachusetts 17901
Office (413) 490-1993 • Home (413) 598-9866 • Fax (413) 598-9867

September 6, 1997

Paul Garber
President
Ryder International
2349 Bonneville Industrial Park, Suite 129
Santa Rosa, CA 98774

Dear Mr. Garber:

Success. I believe it lies in one's ability to merge the strategic with the tactical, to understand the market, to control the finances, and to build a strong management team. No one function is accountable for performance. It is the interrelationship of all core operations and the vision of the leadership team.

Success and improved corporate value is what I have delivered to each of my employers. Through my expertise in operations and logistics management, I have delivered strong performance results:

- Revitalized and rebuilt Epic World's operations, transitioning the organization from a small independent company into a $70+ million corporation with worldwide market penetration. To support our huge growth and expansion, I led over $1 million in technology installations to automate and integrate all core operating, logistics, distribution, transportation and support functions.

- Captured a total of more than $7.5 million in operating cost reductions for Odyssey Distribution, negotiated a multi-million dollar outsourcing contract and personally spearheaded an internal technology "revolution". Through my efforts, the organization was recognized as "best in class" for its operations, logistics and technology infrastructure.

These achievements reflect the quality and caliber of my professional career. What they do not reflect, however, is the strength of my leadership style, my ability to build consensus across operating units, and my contributions to improved revenues, service and profitability.

Now, at this point in my career, I am seeking new professional challenges and opportunities where I can lead the revitalization and expansion of large-scale logistics, transportation, warehousing and distribution operations. If your goal is improved performance, efficiency and cost-savings, we should talk.

Sincerely,

Allen C. Burns

Enclosure

HAROLD C. DAVIS
190 Birchwood Circle
Savannah, Georgia 45452
(912) 323-8752

June 6, 1997

Gerald L. Hampton
President/CEO
Global Logistics, Inc.
3498 Greenwood Avenue
Atlanta, GA 45723

Dear Mr. Hampton:

Building corporate value and improving operating performance is my expertise. As a Senior Operations & Logistics Executive with two major corporations over the past 14 years, I have provided the strategic and tactical leadership instrumental to our profitable growth:

* Revitalized Distribution Systems, transitioning the organization from a small independent company into a $70+ million corporation with worldwide market presence. Personally led $1+ million in technology installations to automate and integrate all core operating, logistics, distribution, transportation and support functions.

* Delivered $7.5 million in operating cost reductions to Arnold Distribution, negotiated a multi-million dollar outsourcing contract and created a "best in class" logistics organization.

* Spearheaded Arnold's initial computerization initiative, investing millions of dollars in technology to automate the entire operating organization with AS/400 platform and multiple software applications.

My performance rests largely in my ability to build consensus across diverse operating functions — from planning, inventory and logistics to field distribution, transportation and customer service/relations. I am decisive in my management style, yet flexible in responding to constantly changing operating, organizational, financial and market demands.

Now, at this point in my career, I am seeking new professional challenges where I can continue to provide strong and decisive operating and logistics leadership. Thus my interest in meeting with you to explore such opportunities with Global Logistics. I appreciate your time in reviewing my qualifications and look forward to speaking with you.

Sincerely,

Harold C. Davis

Enclosure

CHARLES T. MONROE, JR.

104 Maple Drive
Baltimore, Maryland 22412
(410) 949-0987

November 4, 1997

Claude R. Johnson
Vice President - Operations
Millview, Inc.
1644 Edmonds Street
Minneapolis, MN 55347

Dear Mr. Johnson:

For the past nine years, I have planned, staffed and directed large-scale, fully-integrated logistics, warehousing, distribution and transportation operations for Ryder Dedicated Logistics throughout North America. The focus of my career has been divided between start-up operations and the aggressive turn-around/repositioning of existing operations. To each, I have delivered strong and sustainable financial results:

* Built three independent logistics operations for one major customer, from start-up to over $5.5 million in annual revenues to Ryder.

* Led the successful and profitable turnaround of the Challenge Systems logistics operations, implemented training and productivity improvement programs, restored customer credibility and improved financial performance.

Currently, I am orchestrating a complete revitalization of Ryder's operations in Baltimore, an organization fraught with customer dissatisfaction and poor financial performance. In less than nine months, my team and I have re-captured key accounts, improved revenue streams and reduced operating costs. The organization is now positioned for strong growth and expansion.

Although my years with Ryder have been a wonderful experience, I am now ready to pursue new professional challenges. Thus my interest in interviewing as Millview's Director of Logistics. As requested, my recent salary has averaged $95,000 to $125,000 over the past five years.

Sincerely,

Charles T. Monroe, Jr.

Enclosure

MARVIN P. SCHWARTZ
5123 Wedgewood Drive
Huntington, West Virginia 32353
(304) 875-5433

April 15, 1997

Brandon Porter
Executive Vice President
Federal Express
100 Bambridge Avenue
Stamford, CT 16532

Dear Mr. Porter:

Currently a Director with RTM Airways, I am confidentially exploring new professional challenges and would welcome the chance to meet with you to discuss opportunities with Federal Express. My goal is a senior management position requiring strong planning, staffing, budgeting and operating leadership.

With LTM since 1981, I have advanced rapidly and earned significant operating responsibility. In my last position as Regional Service Director, I led a team of 425 in an $80 million operation. Financial results were strong and included a profitable $20 million increase in revenues with better than 6% overall expense reduction.

Based upon my performance, my leadership competencies and my ability to launch innovative projects, I was chosen to direct a nationwide reengineering initiative in 1996. Our goal has been to reduce LTM's reliance on third-party agents and enhance our image within the industry. Again, results have been strong and include a better than 20% cost reduction.

My tenure with RTM has been a wonderful career experience. However, it is now time to explore new opportunities offering greater potential for long-term advancement. As such, my interest in Federal Express and request for a personal interview. Thank you.

Sincerely,

Marvin P. Schwartz

Enclosure

MANUFACTURING

KeyWords, Action Verbs & High-Impact Phrases

To "Nail" Your Cover Letter:

* Productivity & Efficiency Improvements

* Cost Savings & Long-Term Avoidance

* Cross-Functional Team Building & Leadership

* Materials Management & MRP Systems

* Total Quality Management, Quality Assurance & ISO 9000

* Information Technology & Manufacturing Automation

* Process Redesign & Workflow Simplification

* New Plant Start-Up

* Capital & Facilities Improvement

* Product Development & Manufacturability

MAURICE LOVERN
193 Candlers Mountain Road
Little Rock, Arkansas 54321
(227) 325-2778

February 14, 1997

Frank Wright
President
DeWitt, Inc.
9000 West Crescent Square
San Diego, CA 98632

Dear Mr. Wright:

I am a well-qualified Manufacturing Industry Executive successful in building corporate value through my contributions in engineering and production management, quality, performance reengineering, cost control and profit improvement. My expertise lies in my ability to identify core competencies, link with customer demand, and drive forward innovative technology design, manufacturing and delivery programs.

To each start-up venture, turnaround and high-growth company, I provided the strategic and tactical leadership critical to improving financial results. Most notably, I:

* Increased cycle time by 250% and improved product quality by 75% for RON Systems.
* Captured a 35% gain in revenues and 20% gain in profits for another RON facility.
* Implemented state-of-the-art technologies to automate TDR's manufacturing organization.
* Delivered cost reductions averaging 20%+ for Instruments, Inc.
* Spearheaded implementation of ISO 9002, QS9000 and other leading quality certifications.

Never satisfied with the "status quo," I strive to increase performance through a combined program of process redesign, personnel development and customer relationship improvement. In turn, I have consistently achieved financial and operating results well beyond projections, and positioned each organization for long-term growth and accelerated profitability.

I look forward to interviewing as Vice President of Manufacturing. Be advised that I am secure in my current position and wish to remain confidential in my search. Thank you.

Sincerely,

Maurice Lovern

Enclosure

LAWRENCE F. RICE
615 Evergreen Pass
Snake River, Wyoming 61019
(307) 373-5591

January 2, 1997

James Baker
President
Eastern Industrial Services, Inc.
460 Concord Pike
Pottstown, PA 19852

Dear Mr. Baker:

Building corporate value is my expertise. Whether challenged to launch a start-up venture, orchestrate an aggressive turnaround or lead an organization through accelerated growth and expansion, I have consistently delivered strong results:

- As Vice President of Manufacturing for Cooper-Maxwell Corporation, I led a 13-site, 700+ employee organization through a massive change initiative with cost savings projected at more than $4 million and productivity forecasted to improve by a minimum of 10%.

- As Operations Manager with Zortak, I facilitated a complex acquisition and integration of five manufacturing plants into a consolidated business unit, reduced costs by up to 30% at individual plants and participated in closing over $30 million in new sales.

- As Vice President of Operations & Engineering with Craig Associated Industries, my 300-person team delivered the highest production, efficiency, quality and profits in the history of the company.

The strength of my performance lies solely in the diversity of my experience. Unlike most operating executives, my responsibilities have expanded beyond operations to include sophisticated engineering and product development, nationwide sales and customer service, high-level strategic marketing, information technology and the complete human resources function. In fact, my strengths in HR, training and employee relations have been a major catalyst for success throughout my career.

My goal is a senior-level management position with an organization requiring strong and decisive leadership, a real commitment to the workforce, and a vision for long-term growth and expansion. As such, my interest in meeting with you to explore such opportunities with Eastern Industrial Services. Thank you.

Sincerely,

Lawrence F. Rice

Enclosure

153

JACK K. KNIGHTON
1 Brooklawn Drive
Harrison, Ohio 46832

Home (419) 471-5889

Office (419) 471-7500 ext. 122

March 15, 1997

Robert L. Higginbothom
President
Hester Manufacturing
1547 Lexington Avenue
Sikeston, Missouri 63801

Dear Mr. Higginbothom:

When I joined Ryster Wire & Cable as **Operations Manager** in 1994, I was challenged to plan and direct an aggressive reengineering of the facility. To date, my team and I have delivered over $2 million in cost reductions, achieved ISO 9002 certification and supported a 30%+ increase in annual sales. The plant is now considered the flagship operation for the entire division and we are providing process redesign and quality leadership to the entire group.

My previous career experiences and contributions were equally significant:

* As **General Manager** of Lewisman Wire & Cable, I led another successful reorganization and increased profits by 90% over four years.

* As **Manufacturing Operation Manager** for Z-TAP, my team and I improved on-time deliveries by 100%, reduced inventories by more than $2 million and led three successful R&D programs.

* As **Vice President of Manufacturing** for Matric Systems, results included a $1.2 million reduction in WIP and 20% reduction in total production costs.

The value I bring to your organization is not only my track record of performance, but the strong combination of my technical and managerial experience. Anxious to leave Ohio, I am conducting a confidential search through select markets and would welcome the opportunity for a personal interview. My goal is a senior-level operating management position with an organization in need of change, revitalization and aggressive growth.

Thank you.

Sincerely,

Jack K. Knighton

Enclosure

SHIRLEY B. LAWHORN

410 Sandusky Lane
Knoxville, Tennessee 72205
Email: SBL@AOL.COM

Home: (615) 536-5408

Office: (615) 998-0770

May 30, 1997

Kenneth J. Taylor
President & CEO
Stratton Industrial Products, Inc.
908 Baltimore Avenue
Arlington, TX 45332

Dear Mr. Taylor:

Managing large-scale manufacturing operations requires a unique blend of expertise in planning, budgeting, costing, production management, training and staff leadership. It is this core set of competencies I bring to Stratton Industrial Products.

Over the past three years, I have spearheaded an aggressive reorganization and competitive improvement in a unique manufacturing organization operating 118 locations nationwide and employing over 5500 people. My contributions have been strong and include:

- Significant reduction in operating costs and capital expenditures.

- 40% growth over three years.

- Introduction of TQM, productivity management, materials management, safety and other programs that have dramatically increased output, quality and customer satisfaction.

- Development of innovative manufacturing and distribution partnerships with major industry players (e.g., 3M, SC Johnson, Staples).

- Negotiation of more than $350 million in government contracts.

Although secure in my current position, I am confidentially exploring new professional challenges and would welcome the opportunity to interview for the position of Vice President of Manufacturing. My salary requirements can be discussed at the time of our interview. Thank you.

Sincerely,

Shirley B. Lawhorn

Enclosure

CLARENCE E. COATES
125 Mayfield Drive
Wilmington, Delaware 53015
(302) 369-8066

August 15, 1997

Richard Walker
President
Dover Diversified Corporation
1459 Wards Road
Pennsauken, PA 19863

Dear Mr. Walker:

Throughout my 14-year production and operations management career, I have delivered strong performance results through combined expertise in:

- Improving production output. Delivered a 30% yield increase through focused concentration on productivity improvement in core product lines and operations.

- Reducing operating costs. Captured over $250,000 in first year cost savings through a series of production redesign, contract renegotiation and new program/process implementation initiatives.

- Driving quality gains. Championed successful introduction of TQM, continuous improvement, business process reengineering and corporate culture change programs.

- Strengthening union/management relations. Managed sensitive negotiations with union officials to win support for numerous new programs, workforce policies and production initiatives.

In each assignment, my goal has been to improve operations while maintaining the integrity of the business unit, retaining all key personnel, and enhancing our ability to consistently deliver quality service and product. And, I have done so.

Now, at this point in my career, I am seeking new professional challenges where I can continue to lead a high-performance, quality-driven production operation. Thus my interest in meeting with you to explore such opportunities with Dover Diversified. Thank you.

Sincerely,

Clarence E. Coates

Enclosure

JERRY GALLAWAY

207 N. Saratoga
Portland, Oregon 63252

Home (503) 829-9639   Office (503) 594-1700

October 6, 1997

David L. Cameron
President
International Manufacturing, Inc.
1206 Park Street
Oakland, CA 98742

Dear Mr. Cameron:

I am a well-qualified Operating Executive with a strong record of achievement in building corporate value through expertise in:

- Productivity, Efficiency & Quality Improvement
- Cost Reduction & Long-Term Cost Containment
- Revenue & Profit Growth

With more than 15 years' experience, I have built, directed and strengthened manufacturing, production and assembly operations in the U.S., Europe, Russia, Australia and Middle East. This has included independent companies, joint ventures and strategic partnerships. My challenge in each assignment — whether a start-up, turnaround or high-growth venture — has been to develop multinational workforces, introduce new products, create new markets and drive revenue growth.

Please also note that I have strong qualifications in international trade development, import/export and associated international distribution and logistics functions.

The diversity of my products and industry experience is extensive and has allowed me to demonstrate my flexibility in introducing business processes to impact positive change and improved operating performance. Now, at this point in my career, I am seeking the opportunity to transition my experience into a new organization in need of strong and decisive operating leadership.

I would welcome a personal interview to explore management positions with International Manufacturing and look forward to speaking with you.

Sincerely,

Jerry Gallaway

Enclosure

157

BRADLEY G. FOSTER
2013 Poplar Forest Drive
Lexington, Virginia 22071
(540) 986-7167

February 4, 1997

J. Herrmann
Managing Partner
Herrmann Executive Consultants
1007 Broad Street
Philadelphia, PA 11663

Dear Mr. Herrmann:

After a successful career as President, CEO, Vice President and General Manager of diverse manufacturing organizations, I have decided to transition my experience into the consulting arena. My goal is to affiliate with a well-established practice such as Herrmann Executive Consultants, recognized nationwide for their expertise and results.

Just as with consulting, my career has been "project-driven." In addition to my general management and P&L operating unit management responsibilities, I have worked closely with affiliated business units, subsidiaries and divisions to provide expertise on a broad range of operating, financial, marketing, technology and product issues. I have been the crisis manager, troubleshooter and problem solver. For example:

- Assessed status of Rymer's $15 million Canadian Division, identified bottlenecks, redesigned business processes, and realigned staff and management teams. **RESULT:** Transition from $1.3 million loss to $850,000 profit.

- Evaluated efficiency and consolidated nine operating locations into six product-driven organizations. **RESULT:** $2.5 million cost reduction.

- Led corporate relocation to control escalating operating and labor costs. **RESULT:** $2.3 million reduction in labor, benefit, overhead and transportation expenses.

- Introduced leading edge technologies, processes and quality standards (including ISO 9000) to accelerate productivity within labor-intensive operations. **RESULT:** Annual efficiency gains of more than 22%.

- Identified and captured new market opportunities to exploit the core competencies of new business group formed following large corporate merger. **RESULT:** Revenue growth from $59 million to $80 million.

As you can see, I have the project background, operating management skills and capabilities to deliver results for your clients.

I am anxious to speak with you and appreciate your quick response. Please note that I am currently employed and would appreciate your confidentiality in this matter. Thank you.

Sincerely,

Bradley G. Foster

Enclosure

KEVIN LAIRD, JR.
28 Granite Street
Littleton, CO 32033
(303) 654-4533

June 21, 1997

Louis Wesley
President
Langley Production Machinery
1213 Long Meadows
Middleburg, OH 43565

Dear Mr. Wesley:

As **General Manager / Vice President of Manufacturing / Operations Manager**, I have consistently delivered results:

- **30% revenue growth, $1+ million cost reduction and ISO 9002 certification** for Goulder Systems.

- Successful turnaround of Tyler Cable with **90% increase in operating profits and $3 million cost reduction.**

- Accelerated product development program that generated **$5+ million in revenues** for Alloy.

- **$2+ million operating cost reduction** for Bletcher's Powermatic Division.

Throughout my career, I have held full P&L responsibility for Production, R&D, Engineering, Quality, Warehousing, Distribution, Accounting, Human Resources and MIS/Manufacturing Automation. In addition, I have directed staffs of 200+, reengineered workforces to cut costs while optimizing productivity, and provided strong management leadership in start-up, turnaround and high-growth organizations.

My greatest strengths lie in my ability to evaluate existing operations and implement the processes, technologies and systems to improve performance, meet customer objectives and increase bottom-line profitability. Now I am looking for a new opportunity where I can continue to provide strong and decisive leadership.

I would welcome a personal interview to explore management opportunities with Langley Production Machinery and thank you in advance for your consideration.

Sincerely,

Kevin Laird, Jr.

Enclosure

JONATHAN L. ROBBINS
9 Buckingham Place
Bedford, Massachusetts 09863
(508) 564-6543

May 28, 1997

Paul Overstreet
President
Sylvania, Inc.
901 Randolph Street
Edison, NY 14753

Dear Mr. Overstreet:

When I began my professional career with Tremont Products, I thought it was a "quick stop" in manufacturing. Years later and many positions since, I now serve as the **Vice President of Production & Distribution**. My challenge was to reengineer the entire logistics process. The results:

- $1+ million cost reduction.
- 75% increase in production output.
- $1+ million capital investment to meet customer demand.

My achievements during my tenure with the Personal Products Company were just as significant and included:

- $2+ million in cost savings.
- $40 million in sales volume for start-up manufacturing line.
- 50% reduction in product damage and 60% reduction in workplace safety incidents.

Recognized by my peers for excellence in operations management, team building, work flow optimization and customer satisfaction, I have tackled each new assignment with a keen focus not only on cost reduction, but also process redesign, productivity improvement and performance gain. In turn, financial results have been significant for start-up ventures, turnarounds and high-growth corporations.

Now, at this venture in my career, I am looking to take the "next step." My goal is a senior-level management position where I can continue to provide strong and decisive operating leadership, while expanding the scope of my responsibilities into sales, marketing and finance.

I look forward to speaking with you about such opportunities and appreciate your time and consideration. Thank you.

Sincerely,

Jonathan L. Robbins

Enclosure

160

MANFRED A. YOUNG
111 Buxton Avenue
Richmond, Virginia 26533
(804) 666-0738

September 5, 1997

Charles F. Zimmerman
President
Hoover Manufacturing, Inc.
173 Oak Street
Richmond, VA 25335

Dear Mr. Zimmerman:

I need your help!

In discussing my situation with several colleagues in the area, your name has repeatedly come to my attention as someone who would be of invaluable assistance. Knowing that your time is quite limited, I will be brief.

I moved to Richmond to join the Palmer Company as their new Vice President of Marketing & Operations. Within less than two years, I reduced costs by more than 28% and delivered a 6% gain in productivity. Long-term revenue results are strong and the company is poised for aggressive growth.

Recently, I resigned my position for a number of reasons that we can discuss. However, my family and I are anxious to remain in the area, and as such, I am seeking your advice regarding my resume and job search. The majority of my career has been in consumer products (including nine years with Coca-Cola). Several opportunities have already presented themselves, but I am anxious to find the "best" opportunity in the region.

Mr. Zimmerman, I would like to schedule a brief meeting with you to get any feedback and guidance you can offer. I will phone on Tuesday to arrange a convenient time and promise to be brief and to the point.

Thank you. Your reputation in the region is obviously significant and your input would be appreciated.

Kind regards,

Manfred A. Young

Enclosure

MANAGEMENT INFORMATION SYSTEMS

KeyWords, Action Verbs & High-Impact Phrases

To "Nail" Your Cover Letter:

* New Media, Internet & Online Technologies

* Client/Server & Database Technology

* Telecommunications Technology

* Process Redesign & Automation

* Software Acquisition & Customization

* User Training & Support

* Operating Cost Reductions

* Technology Outsourcing

* Systems Design & New Technology Development

* Information Systems Technology

HENRY WALTERS

3278 Walnut Circle
Revere, Connecticut 16637
(860) 647-3147

December 1, 1997

Joseph Howard
Senior Vice President
Digital Equipment Corporation
1990 Colonial Avenue, Suite 2383
Boston, MA 01748

Dear Mr. Howard:

Developing innovative technology and networking solutions is my expertise. As a Director of Engineering and Engineering Manager with Maxwell, Duncan, and several technology start-up ventures, I have provided the strategic, technical and operational leadership critical to our market success.

Highlights of my career that may be of particular interest to you include:

* Currently spearheading the development of world class network systems monitoring and management technologies for deployment worldwide.
* Guided Duncan's development of advanced client/server applications for the manufacturing industry in cooperation with major partners (e.g., Honeywell, GE, TI, Allen Bradley, Fisher).
* Created some of the industry's first-ever network performance management, characterization, testing and analysis tools, providing distinct competitive advantages for both internal and external applications.
* Built and led new engineering and R&D organizations through development, staffing, funding and operations.

My greatest strength lies in my ability to evaluate technology requirements, integrating the personnel and resources critical to systems development, operability and marketability. Further, I have excellent qualifications in technical marketing, partner relationships and long-range systems/strategic planning.

Currently I am exploring new engineering management opportunities and would welcome a personal interview at your convenience. I appreciate your time and look forward to speaking with you.

Sincerely,

Henry Walters

Enclosure

BLAKE ISLEY

13906 1st Street
San Francisco, California 94102

Phone: (415) 477-3255
Email: bisley@indigo.com

March 15, 1997

Matthew Gilliam
Director of Human Resources
Godsey's Telesystems, Inc.
952 Main Street, Suite 122
Menlo Park, CA 97421

Dear Mr. Gilliam:

Technological excellence and success. It lies in one's ability to merge the strategic with the tactical, to understand the needs and expectations of each organization, and to deliver and support the technologies and applications appropriate to each functional organization.

As **Director of Information Systems & Technology / Assistant CIO** for several organizations, I have provided the technological and organizational leadership that has delivered such success. Under my direction:

- Quincy's global IS function has undergone an evolution and is now operating as a worldwide class organization with advanced information, networking and telecommunications operations with 99% systems availability.

- California Association for the Disabled is now one of the most sophisticated in the nationwide organization with exceptional quality ratings, advanced enterprise and networking technologies, and again, a consistent 99% systems availability.

My role in each organization has been to re-create, rebuild and expand IS competencies through both internal development and external acquisition initiatives. The strength of my personal technology skills is excellent. However, more important have been my contributions to the vision, strategy and long-range development of IS organizations that not only capture new technologies but support rapid changes in operations and business demands.

Now, at this point in my career, I am seeking new professional challenges and opportunities, and would welcome a personal interview at your earliest convenience. Thank you.

Sincerely,

Blake Isley

Enclosure

WILLIAM JONES
1250 Scribe Street
Los Angeles, California 94003
Home (310) 928-4850   Office (310) 226-0500

May 31, 1997

Ralph Machianno
President
Netware, Inc.
12000 West Boulevard, Suite 123
Menlo Park, CA 98323

Dear Mr. Machianno:

When I joined Conrad Computer in 1994, I was challenged to re-create and strengthen the internal world-wide computing function for the corporation. Within less than two years, my team and I:

* Improved system availability to 99.5%.
* Built a proactive partnership between application development and operations.
* Transitioned to UNIX architecture.
* Met/exceeded all budget, quality and performance goals.

Previously, during my 7-year career with ART, Inc., I introduced automated MIS operations, brought troubled projects "back on track" and cost-effectively managed a 150-person datacenter operation. Earlier career experience focused on the design, development and delivery of Tandem systems technology.

The combination of my experience in systems operations, applications development, telecommunications and performance management has allowed me to deliver results despite often complex challenges. My technological capabilities are complemented by strong training and leadership skills and a long-standing commitment to productivity and performance improvement.

Although secure in my position with Conrad, I am confidentially exploring new management opportunities where I can continue to lead a top-flight technology organization through change, refinement and improvement. As such, my interest in Netware, Inc. and request for a personal interview. Thank you.

Sincerely,

William Jones

Enclosure

MARY C. CAMPBELL
300 South Windsor Avenue
New Haven, Connecticut 20316

Home (860) 949-8430   Office (860) 565-7316

October 8, 1997

Lyle Berkstein
President
Apple Computer
1239 Microchip Road
Silicon Valley, CA 98323

Dear Mr. Berkstein:

I am a well-qualified Information Technology Executive successful in identifying organizational needs and leading the development/implementation of emerging technologies to improve productivity, quality and operating performance. Most recently, I have focused my efforts on introducing document imaging technologies as part of First System's corporate-wide vision for developing and managing departmental client/server systems.

The scope of my responsibility has included the entire project management cycle, from initial needs assessment and technology evaluations through vendor selection, internal systems development, pilot testing, quality review, technical and user documentation, and full-scale implementation. Most notable are my strengths in facilitating cooperation among cross-functional project teams to ensure that all projects are delivered on time, within budget and as per specifications.

The strength of my experience (largely acquired through my years in the banking industry) is easily transferrable across industries. My role as IS project manager is not bound by function, but rather by success in responding to the vastly different operating needs of sales, marketing, finance, purchasing, legal, regulatory affairs, administration and other core business units.

Although secure in my current position, I am confidentially exploring new opportunities. My goal is a top-level IS management position where I can continue to provide strong and effective leadership in technology development and solutions engineering.

I look forward to a personal interview and thank you in advance for your consideration.

Sincerely,

Mary C. Campbell

Enclosure

BRENDA WILLIAMSON

235 Costal Highway
Sunset Beach, Florida 33137-5319
(954) 858-4847

October 18, 1997

President
Intertechnology Manufacturing
1290 Glenview Drive
Chicago, IL 60610

Dear Sir/Madam:

Aware of the fast-track growth of your organization and the advances in technology you have delivered, I am writing to express my interest in senior-level project management opportunities. Highlights of my professional career include:

- Over 15 years' experience leading complex design, engineering and field project management teams.

- Outstanding technical, engineering, design, analytical and contract administration qualifications.

- Leadership of up to 50-person cross-functional project teams working cooperatively to achieve common goals and performance objectives.

- Consistent success in delivering projects on time and within budget (many ahead of schedule and well below forecasted costs).

- Negotiation of large-dollar, multi-year design, engineering and service contracts that have strengthened market position and accelerated revenue growth.

The core of my experience is in the utility, construction and food processing industries, each with unique technological, engineering and project management requirements. My goal is to remain within one of these industries where I believe my experience and competencies are of most value.

I would welcome the opportunity to speak with you regarding your current management requirements and appreciate both your time and consideration of my qualifications. Thank you.

Sincerely,

Brenda Williamson

Enclosure

SHARON RIVIERA
1281 Meadows Drive
Thomaston, Georgia 30368
Home (706) 642-4140   Office (706) 652-5159

October 22, 1997

Ms. Jill Klein
David C. Cooper & Associates
5 Concourse Parkway, Suite 2700
Atlanta, GA 30328

Dear Ms. Klein:

In my current position as Group Information Resources Controller with Border Inc., I direct a high-profile corporate finance function responsible for all information technologies, resources, assets and operations in 50 IS departments throughout the global business organization. My challenge has been to create a formal financial infrastructure to control our IS efforts and ensure that our investments in technology are appropriate, cost-effective and responsive to our needs.

Results have been significant and served as the cornerstone for our tremendous strides in IS capabilities over the past several years. Just as notable are my contributions to process design, strategic planning for performance improvement, and cost reduction ($1+ million projected in vendor savings).

With a total of 10 years' experience in corporate accounting, finance and audit, combined with strong qualifications in IS technology, I bring to a new organization demonstrated competence in jointly managing both business functions. Just as critical, however, is my ability to link these operations with the core business to achieve our strategic, tactical and profit goals.

Now, at this point in my career, I am confidentially exploring new professional challenges and opportunities where I can continue to drive forward both finance and IS operations. As such, if you are working with a client company in need of strong management leadership, I would welcome the chance to pursue the position and appreciate both your time and consideration. Thank you.

Sincerely,

Sharon Riviera

Enclosure

ROBERT ZUCKERMAN
950 Inglewood Drive
Malvern, Pennsylvania 19104

Home (610) 332-2130   Work (610) 324-2056

DATE

James Ryan
President
Georgia Pacific Corporation
1400 Peach Tree Lane
Atlanta, GA 30330

Dear Mr. Ryan:

I am currently employed as the Director of Information Services for a 3600-employee organization. Recruited in 1994, my goal has been to upgrade the technology architecture and drive forward aggressive initiatives to expand competencies, systems and applications throughout the organization. To date, our results have been impressive, including transition to client/server, TCP/IP frame relay, Novell LAN, data warehousing, decision support and Internet technology tools. Further, we have captured over $10 million in development and operating cost reductions.

This assignment is reflective of the quality and caliber of my entire professional career — identify opportunities to develop/acquire new technologies that will have an immediate impact upon core business operations and support long-range corporate operating and financial goals.

During my tenure with the U.S. Army, I followed a unique career path reserved specifically for individuals demonstrating unique technical and leadership expertise.   Working hand-in-hand with top senior executives, I guided the development of technologies impacting personnel worldwide. Most notably, I led the implementation of emerging technologies into existing IT organizations to further strengthen technical, organizational and leadership competencies.

Now, at this point in my career, I am seeking new challenges and opportunities. My goal is a senior-level IT management position where I can guide the acquisition, development and operations of an advanced technology group. As such, my interest in meeting with you to explore such opportunities with Georgia Pacific.

I look forward to speaking with you and thank you for your consideration.

Sincerely,

Robert Zuckerman

Enclosure

MARKETING

KeyWords, Action Verbs & High-Impact Phrases

To "Nail" Your Cover Letter:

* New Product & Technology Launches

* New Market Penetration

* Strategic Alliances & Co-Marketing

* Joint Ventures

* Product Lifecycle Management

* Cross-Functional Team Leadership

* Market, Industry & Trend Analysis

* Competitive Market Intelligence

* Strategic Market Planning & Positioning

* Product Development & Pricing

DIANE C. NOVAK
121 Seaport Lane
Bangor, Maine 08763

Home (207) 762-7440

Office (207) 594-8168

June 8, 1997

Alexander McDaniel
President
Moody, Inc.
2229 Yorktown Avenue
Wilmington, Delaware 19803

Dear Mr. McDaniel:

Creating successful marketing programs is more of a challenge than ever before. With the advent of multiple electronic technologies, in tandem with the already existing marketing channels, a Marketing Director is faced with unlimited options for business development. My success lies in my ability to evaluate each of these channels, determine the most appropriate mix of marketing tools, and create the campaigns that deliver results.

Throughout my professional career, I have facilitated the strategic planning, development and implementation of marketing programs designed to accelerate base business while launching the introduction of numerous new products, services and technologies. My ability to build and lead cross-functional teams of creative design, marketing and management personnel has been critical to our performance.

In my current position, I assumed responsibility for leading the marketing organization through a period of rapid growth and expansion to meet the needs of an aggressive corporate sales organization. To date, our results have been significant and include growth from a virtual start-up to our current position with almost $1 billion in revenues. My marketing programs have been instrumental in this performance.

Now, at this point in my career, I am seeking new professional challenges where I can continue to provide strategic, tactical and creative marketing leadership. As such, my interest in meeting with you to explore opportunities with Moody. Thank you.

Sincerely,

Diane C. Novak

Enclosure

WARREN A. BAKER
1620 Meridith Court
Omaha, Nebraska 21753
Email: wbaker@yatzman.com
Phone: (402) 331-0657

November 21, 1997

Howard T. Peyton
President
ElectraData, Inc.
3609 Surrey Avenue
Port Jefferson, NY 11777

Dear Mr. Peyton:

Whether challenged to lead an aggressive market expansion into emerging domestic and international market sectors, launch the start-up of a new business unit or introduce innovative market programs to realign a national sales organization, I have achieved measurable results:

- **As Vice President of New Business Development**, spearheaded Yatzman America's successful market launch into the digital consumer products industry delivering $5.2 million in revenues in first month and $150 million potential revenue stream within five years.

- **As General Manager for Occid's Electronic Imaging Department**, led the start-up of new business unit, guided development of more than nine multimedia, information technologies/products, and drove revenues to $11 million within three years.

- **As National Sales Manager with Closman Products**, championed the introduction of quality, productivity and performance improvement initiatives to restructure and realign the sales organization. Gained a significant competitive advantage and captured key accounts nationwide.

My strengths lie in my ability to conceive and implement the strategic action plans to identify new market opportunities, develop state-of-the-art technologies/products and negotiate strategic partnerships to drive global market expansion and revenue/profit growth. Equally notable, are my strong qualifications in general management, P&L management, financial affairs, recruitment and training.

Now, I am seeking a senior-level sales or management position with a high-growth technology development organization where I can continue to provide strong and decisive sales/management leadership. I would welcome a personal interview explore such an assignment with ElectraData. Thank you for your time and consideration.

Sincerely,

Warren A. Baker

Enclosure

BRYAN CAMPBELL
4551 South 45th Street, Apt. 2B
New York, NY 10054
(212) 654-6547

October 2, 1997

Sable Tillman
HR Director
Enterprise Magazine
130 5th Avenue
New York, NY 10011-4399

Dear Ms. Tillman:

I spoke with one of your personnel associates the other day (Natalie Greenstreet) who suggested I forward my resume in response to your advertisement for a Market Research Manager. Highlights of my professional career that may be of particular interest to you include the following:

- More than 10 years' experience in the Print Publishing Industry.

- Proven success in enhancing a publication's image through well-targeted and well-executed marketing and public relations efforts.

- Excellent research, data collection, data synthesis and documentation skills.

- Extensive network of contacts with local government officials, civic and business leaders, and the media throughout the New York metro area.

- Strong background in ad sales, lead generation, customer/advertiser relations and copyrighting/editing.

- Ability to independently plan, prioritize and manage special projects.

- Outstanding skills and competencies in editorial content development.

My goal is to transition my experience into a high-profile market research management position where I can continue to drive forward growth and market recognition for a specialty advertiser. You will find that the combination of my research, writing and project management qualifications will make a positive and long-lasting impact upon the success of Enterprise Magazine.

I appreciate your time and consideration, and look forward to meeting with you. My salary requirements are flexible. Thank you.

Sincerely,

Bryan Campbell

Enclosure

LISA SPRINGER

34 Smith Road
Lewisville, Arkansas 20347

Home: (761) 676-9322
Email: lisaannspring@aol.com

July 1, 1997

Patti Howard, Associate
Heidrick & Struggles, Inc.
300 South Grand Avenue
Suite 2400
Los Angeles, CA 90071-1685

Dear Ms. Howard:

It is with great interest that I forward my resume for consideration as Senior Vice President of Marketing and Development. With more than 17 years' experience in marketing (the past seven of which have been concentrated in new media and cable broadcast), I bring to the position a unique blend of creative, strategic and management talents of significant value to the organization.

Currently, as the Senior Vice President and Group Account Director for Foundation Communications and its principal business units (including emerging online and multimedia technologies), I spearhead a dynamic media marketing organization. My challenge has been to expand and strengthen market presence through the introduction of a diversified portfolio of advertising, business development, promotional and strategic alliance initiatives. Results have been significant and include:

- Capture of an 11% gain in overall primetime cable share.
- Creation of "standardized" programming and scheduling to attract and retain a loyal audience.
- Development of innovative multimedia advertising and promotional strategies.
- Expansion into new media applications.

Just as significant has been my management success in building and leading cross-functional teams, merging the critical functions of marketing, advertising, research, sales, distribution and creative programming. Further, I have instilled a sense of entrepreneurial vision and creativity to drive forward innovative strategies to win competitive positioning and accelerate revenue growth.

Although secure in my current position, I am confidentially exploring new opportunities where I can direct a large-scale marketing initiative on behalf of a cable/broadcast/media organization. Thus my interest in the Game Show Network and your search for a Senior Vice President of Marketing & Development. I look forward to a personal interview. Thank you.

Sincerely,

Lisa Springer

Enclosure

174

JEFFERSON YOST

4584 Franklin Bridge Court
Bell Tavern, Idaho 67882

Home   (416) 478-7724
Office (416) 982-5294
Fax   (416) 473-1510

June 24, 1997

Paul Mitchell
President
Mitchell Capital Investments
714 Orchard Street
Stockton, CA 95219

Dear Mr. Mitchell:

Building corporate value is my expertise. Whether challenged to launch a start-up venture, accelerate revenues within a high-growth organization or spearhead a successful turnaround, I have consistently delivered strong and sustainable financial results:

- Growth from start-up to over $16 million in revenues for Colorstone.
- Growth from start-up to over $6 million in revenues for MacLeod & Maxwell.
- Turnaround of the Consumer Products Division and transition to the #1 profit producer in American Energy Associates (AEA).
- Transition from $350,000 in export sales to over $6 million in annual sales for AEA.

These achievements are indicative of the quality and caliber of my entire professional career - identify and capitalize upon opportunities to build new markets, generate new revenue streams and outperform competition in both domestic and international markets.

With more than 15 years' experience in consumer products, forest products, manufacturing and whole-sale distribution, I bring a wealth of success in these markets. Most significant are my established relationships with major retail chains throughout the U.S. I know the people, the products, the merchandising strategies and the operations of these retailers. In turn, I have been successful in building sales partnerships that have been profitable for both the retail organizations and my employers.

I look forward to speaking with you regarding senior management opportunities and appreciate your consideration. Be assured that the strength of my operating experience, entrepreneurial drive and commitment to success will add measurable value to your operations.

Sincerely,

Jefferson Yost

Enclosure

FRANKLIN J. REED
512 Landon Avenue
Cooperton, Maine 35488
(305) 544-1054

March 8, 1997

Kenneth J. Cress
President
Cress Equity Partners
1900 Madison Avenue, 14th Floor
New York, NY 10015

Dear Mr. Cress :

Throughout my Marketing career, I have provided strong and decisive leadership to challenging start-up, turnaround and high-growth companies. My expertise lies in my ability to identify opportunities, define strategic goals and vision, and lead tactical implementation. Results are significant and include:

- Transitioning a new marketing organization and product line from concept through start-up to over $100 million in annual volume.

- Realigning and expanding third party distribution network, capturing 20% revenue growth and strengthening competitive market position.

- Introducing innovative marketing, business development and promotional strategies that accelerated growth within existing business units and delivered revenues beyond projections.

- Negotiating strategic alliances and partnerships to accelerate market growth.

- Evaluating merger, acquisition and joint ventures opportunities to expand product portfolios and gain competitive advantages.

My industry experience is diverse including, but not limited to, banking/financial services, consumer products, packaged goods, publishing, health care and food commodities. My ability to transcend my marketing expertise into vastly different industries clearly demonstrates my flexibility and ease in understanding the unique marketing characteristics of these specific industries, markets and customer bases.

Now, at this point in my career, I am interested in new professional challenges where I can continue to provide strong and decisive marketing leadership. Knowing that the venture capital community offers unique opportunities, I have focused my search in such a direction and would welcome a personal interview at your earliest convenience. Thank you.

Sincerely,

Franklin J. Reed

Enclosure

MARCUS ANDREWS
100 Windsor Place
Evington, Illinois 55463
(217) 355-5453

March 31, 1997

Clyde T. Dorsey
Senior Partner
Capital Investments
2800 President's Avenue, Suite 106
Great Falls, VA 22066-4106

Dear Mr. Dorsey:

I'm looking for a unique executive opportunity where I can provide strong, decisive and market-driven leadership. My goal is not the "status quo," but rather an emerging, high-growth or turnaround organization that requires an individual with vision, and just as significant, the ability to translate that vision into meaningful action.

My career has accelerated based upon my ability to deliver results despite financial, market and organizational challenges. As you review the enclosed resume, you will be introduced to what I consider some of my most significant accomplishments — revenue and profit gains, long-term cost reductions and critical performance reengineering initiatives.

What distinguishes me from other executives are my strengths in:

- Identifying and capitalizing upon market opportunities to drive growth, expansion and diversification.

- Exploiting an organization's core competencies to gain competitive market advantages.

- Creating vital sales, marketing and service organizations unmatched in customer satisfaction and retention.

- Combining all critical management functions — strategic planning, finance, marketing, product launch, administration, executive development and multi-site operations.

- Negotiating favorable partnerships, strategic alliances and joint ventures.

If positive and improved ROI are your objectives, please call.

Sincerely,

Marcus Andrews

Enclosure

MARVIN K. DELANEY
1104 Jackson Street
Birmingham, Alabama 54734
(205) 347-4269

August 5, 1997

Bruce J. Carrington
Senior Vice President
Leech & Hicks, Inc.
3945 Westgate Avenue
Grand Rapids, MI 48375

Dear Mr. Carrington:

Building corporate value and delivering sustained revenue growth is my expertise. Whether challenged to launch a new business venture or product line, turnaround a non-performing business unit, or accelerate growth within a well-established corporation, I have consistently delivered results:

* 12% revenue gain for Desmond Corporation and transition from product sales to market-driven solution systems company.
* Transition from loss to profitability with $7 million revenue growth for RRT Corporation.
* Creation of new national product category for Rimer's Magic Gel, the most profitable category in the company's history.

Critical to my marketing success are my strengths in strategic planning, market shift assessment and response, action planning and personnel training. In each organization, I have created the sales and service training programs that have supported the business plan and provided the foundation for tremendous market growth. With Diversey, my sales and service training programs immediately returned a large sales region from loss to profitability and have continued to strengthen our field performance.

At this point in my career, I have decided to explore new professional challenges and opportunities. Thus my interest in Leech & Hicks and your need for talented, decisive and results-driven sales, marketing and/or training leadership.

I look forward to speaking with you and will phone next week to arrange a mutually convenient time. Thank you.

Sincerely,

Marvin K. Delaney

Enclosure

178

LEO WOOD
225 Coffee Road
Middleridge, Texas 98731
Email LEOW@AOL.com

Home (817) 695-8962   Office (817) 274-4197

November 2, 1997

Ernest Holland
President
Jefferson Franklin, Inc.
507 Church Street
Milwaukee, WI 53072

Dear Mr. Holland:

Recruited as National Marketing Manager with a Fortune 200 company in 1994, I was challenged to build a high-profile business development function to enter the emerging education market. To date, I have doubled sales to hundreds of millions in dollars annually and strengthened our competitive position. Most notably, I:

- Expanded and strengthened direct and distributor sales networks.
- Personally closed multimillion dollar sales with top executives.
- Created an innovative customer profiling and targeting system.
- Provided strong and decisive sales leadership.
- Introduced Internet technology, established a virtual office environment and significantly reduced the cost of sales.

My strength lies in my ability to identify market opportunity, merge strategy with tactical action and deliver results.

Please note that I have strong general management qualifications in strategic planning, human resources, training/development, budgeting and operations.

I am confidentially exploring new professional opportunities and would welcome the chance to interview as National Marketing Director. My salary requirements are $200,000+.

Sincerely,

Leo Wood

Enclosure

MARGARET PAISLEY

320 Warwick Drive
Sunnyvale, California 97312
(213) 435-5928
mpaisley@att.net

January 31, 1997

Rebecca Bronson
Columbia Executive Search
P.O. Box 1293
Reston, Virginia 20194-1293

Dear Ms. Bronson:

I am an eight-year veteran of AT&T's marketing organization and the recognized leader of several of the corporation's most successful and most profitable new business development initiatives. Promoted rapidly throughout my tenure, I have delivered strong and sustainable gains in market performance and revenue growth within diverse market segments. Most notably, I:

- Created value-added marketing opportunities to accelerate AT&T's presence within the retail industry through a unique partnership with Price Club. **RESULTS**: Current projections forecast $300 million in first year revenues following full-scale launch of AT&T Marketplace.

- Spearheaded development of AT&T's marketing efforts to expand penetration throughout colleges and universities nationwide. **RESULTS**: Development of new, top-performing, 50-person sales and marketing organization generating a $30 million increase in sales revenues within first year.

- Led development of new marketing organization to expand AT&T's success within the Federal Government sector and then personally directed high-profile sales and business development initiatives. **RESULTS**: Closed over $12.8 million in new business contracts and delivered record pipeline activity.

These achievements are indicative of the quality and caliber of my entire professional career — identify and capitalize upon emerging market opportunities within the telecommunications industry to drive forward strong growth and outpace the competition. Now, at this point in my career, I am seeking new professional challenges and opportunities where I can continue to develop, nurture and deliver profitable new markets.

If you are working with a client company seeking a high-energy, high-performance marketing executive, I would welcome the opportunity for a personal interview. Be advised that I am open to relocation and that my salary requirements are $100,000+. Thank you.

Sincerely,

Margaret Paisley

Enclosure

180

PRODUCT DEVELOPMENT

KeyWords, Action Verbs & High-Impact Phrases

To "Nail" Your Cover Letter:

* New Product Research & Development

* New Product Market Launch

* Pricing & Profitability Analysis

* Product Lifecycle Management

* Market & Customer Research & Product Needs Analysis

* Revenue Generation

* Market Share Ratings

* Co-Development Alliances & Joint Ventures

* Cross-Functional Engineering Teams

* Quality Testing & Performance Management

DAVID RICHARDS
5140 Deer Runn
Grand Rapids, Michigan 63202
Residence (616) 475-7188
Business (616) 594-6000 x254

January 5, 1997

Ms. Josephine Winters
Vice President of Human Resources
New Image Technologies, Inc.
1847 Goodwin Avenue
Marietta, GA 32332

Dear Ms. Winters:

As Vice President / Director of Product Development for Communication Guide Associates, I was credited with the conceptualization, technical/engineering development, prototyping and global market launch of more than 10 new products during my tenure. Currently, these products generate over $30 million in annual sales revenues and have further strengthened the corporation's position as the world-wide leader in computer communication software and hardware products.

My performance and success in product development is due largely to my ability to manage cross-functional project teams, building consensus across diverse business disciplines to achieve common development, marketing and profit objectives. Equally notable is my strength in evaluating market opportunities, understanding customer needs, and winning executive-level support and financing to advance technology development.

Of particular note was my selection to spearhead CGA's largest and most strategic single development project in the history of the company. This effort, launched through a joint partnership with Microsoft, is projected to generate over $50 million in new revenues over the next four years. Most recently, as Vice President of Engineering for Clybord Electronics, I created the corporation's first formal engineering organization and delivered a 35% cost savings through innovative process redesign and technology.

Now, at this point in my career, I am seeking new professional challenges and opportunities where I can again provide strong, decisive and market-driven leadership to a diverse product/technology development team. Aware of your commitment to new product development, I would be delighted to meet with you to explore my potential value and contributions to New Image Technologies. Thank you.

Sincerely,

David Richards

Enclosure

CARL STEPHENSON

1432 Blue Jay Way
Nashua, New Hampshire 04450

Home (446) 425-7656
Office (446) 277-1506

February 25, 1997

Jeffrey Samson
President
3M Corporation
1000 Industrial Way
Minneapolis, MN 55463

Dear Mr. Samson:

Throughout my professional career in R&D, product development and product commercialization, I have led the design, pilot testing, scale-up and transition to full-scale production of more than nine new products and line extensions that have delivered millions of dollars in new revenues. My expertise lies in my ability to translate market demand into functional product to meet the needs of users nationwide.

For the past seven years, my challenge has been to accelerate product development for Russell's Printing and Publishing Systems Division. To date, my team and I have introduced three major products/line extensions, each with significant financial gain. Equally notable has been my success in redesigning existing products to increase functionality, improve quality and reduce manufacturing costs.

On a more personal note, I have been repeatedly recognized throughout the Russell organization for my creativity, innovation and product success. I enjoy challenge and am now looking for a new professional opportunity. Thus my interest in 3M and request for a personal interview.

Thank you for your time and your consideration. I look forward to speaking with you.

Sincerely,

Carl Stephenson

Enclosure

ALLEN TEMPLETON
7336 Riverfront Drive
Gardenview, Missouri 60627
(787) 796-3958

September 15, 1997

David Weinert
Chief Operating Officer
Seipold Technologies, Inc.
1900 South 5th Avenue
New York, NY 10010

Dear Mr. Weinert:

Throughout my professional career, I have planned and directed more than 35 technology design and development projects. With full responsibility for the entire project cycle, I have led teams of up to 35 hardware, software and electronics engineers delivering state-of-the-art computer, electronics and test technology.

Most notable have been my achievements in managing both fast-track design projects as well as projects requiring significant technical, scheduling and cost changes. To each, I have delivered strong project leadership and consistently exceeded all performance results.

Please also note that I have strong qualifications in customer management, customer technical presentations, technical training, technical documentation, proposal development and project budgeting. I am direct and decisive in my management style, yet flexible in responding to constantly changing project, customer and business demands.

At this point in my career, I am exploring new management opportunities in program/project management, and would welcome a personal interview at your earliest convenience. Thank you.

Sincerely,

Allen Templeton

Enclosure

PURCHASING & MATERIALS MANAGEMENT

KeyWords, Action Verbs & High-Impact Phrases

To "Nail" Your Cover Letter:

* Vendor & Supplier Relations

* Cost Savings

* Supply Chain Management

* MRP Technology & Systems

* Vendor Sourcing & Contract Negotiations

* Inventory Planning & Management

* Warehousing & Distribution

* Asset & Resource Management

* Competitive Bidding & Contract Award

* Vendor Quality Review & Management

PAUL A. SHELBY

141 Roundabout Drive
Morrison Township, Arkansas 83415

Home (554) 566-1285
Office (554) 358-5870

September 4, 1997

Charles Abbington
Vice President of Operations
Becthold Corporation
293 Washington Avenue
Dallas, TX 87451

Dear Mr. Abbington:

With 12 years' experience in purchasing management and material/supply sourcing, I bring to your organization strong qualifications and a record of consistent achievement in:

* Negotiating multi-million dollar, multi-year purchasing contracts — long-term, fixed price and minority supplier.
* Identifying quality suppliers and establishing favorable pricing, terms and conditions.
* Transferring supply contracts from foreign to domestic sources to meet stringent quality and performance requirements.
* Directing sophisticated manufacturing engineering and tooling programs.

Most notably, I have captured millions of dollars in cost savings, including:

* $20 million purchasing cost reduction for Venture Systems.
* $5.5 million purchasing cost reduction for Chrysler Corporation.

I am most proud of my tenure with Venture Systems. Recruited in 1991, I built the organization's purchasing function from concept into a 10-person worldwide business unit responsible for over $550 million in annual procurement acquisitions. Our financial and operational successes were notable and included the introduction of innovative business strategies, procurement policies and strategic vendor alliances.

Currently, I am exploring new professional opportunities and would welcome a personal interview as Vice President of Purchasing. Thank you.

Sincerely,

Paul A. Shelby

Enclosure

JONAS GREEN
567 Renaldi Avenue
Greensboro, North Carolina 38989
(989) 383-2843

March 19, 1997

Anthony Lebowitz
Plant Manager
IDS Plastics Incorporated
P.O. Box 389
Denver, CO 30090

Dear Mr. Lebowitz:

Please accept this letter and enclosed resume as application for the position of Materials Manager as advertised in the Denver Post. In summary,

Your Requirements	My Qualifications
10 Years' Materials Experience	13 years of increasingly responsible experience in Purchasing, Materials Management, Contracts & Outsourcing
Expertise in MRP & JIT	Planned and directed the acquisition, integration and management of four new MRP/MRP II, JIT and SPC systems. Results included a better than 42% reduction in annual material expenditures.
Leadership Competency	Direct responsibility for the recruitment, training and supervision of up to 120 professional, labor and administrative support staff.
Performance Improvement	Track record of consistent gains in productivity, quality, efficiency and cost reduction in both turnaround and high-growth manufacturing and distribution organizations.
PC Proficiency	Proficient with Lotus, Excel, Schedule+, ACT and Word.

After more than five years on the East Coast, I am anxious to return to the Denver area (where I was educated and worked the first eight years of my career). In fact, I am quite familiar with the operations at IDS and have known Bill Black and Paul Gates for most of my life. As such, I understand the culture of the environment and your long-term objectives.

I look forward to meeting you and can travel to Denver at your convenience. As requested, my salary requirements are in the $95,000 to $115,000 range, but are negotiable based upon the specific scope of responsibility of the position. Thank you.

Sincerely,

Jonas Green

Enclosure

187

QUALITY

KeyWords, Action Verbs & High-Impact Phrases

To "Nail" Your Cover Letter:

* Quality Assurance

* Total Quality Management (TQM)

* Product Staging & Testing

* New Product Development

* ISO 9000 & ISO 14000

* Process Redesign & Documentation

* Quality Circles & Quality Teams

* Cost Savings

* Profit Gains

* Manufacturing & Service Quality

SIMON GARFIELD

4463 South Vine Street
Allentown, Pennsylvania 18755
(610) 656-6563

June 6, 1997

Eugene Robinson
President
Deibold Inc.
9834 Westinghouse Way
Pittsburgh, PA 18761

Dear Mr. Robinson:

Building high performance, quality-driven organizations is my expertise!

Throughout my professional career, I have led the design, development and implementation of sophisticated quality assurance and quality management programs that have consistently strengthened operating and financial performance. The range of my actions has transcended virtually all business functions — from advanced manufacturing and production to executive office functions. To each organization, I delivered strong results. Most notably I:

*   Spearheaded development of an organization-wide TQM program for Kreister's Safety Restraint Systems, led 100+ project teams and delivered millions in annual cost savings.

*   Championed development and transfer of Total Quality Leadership program from US into European and Latin American operations.

*   Introduced sophisticated reengineering processes, technical training programs, quality incentives, work standards and other performance-driven tools to improve operations and facilitate positive change.

Please also note that I have strong analytical, project management, team building, organizational and interpersonal skills. I lead by action and have delivered tremendous gains in total employee involvement and ownership.

Currently, I am exploring new professional opportunities in Quality Management/Quality Assurance and would welcome a personal interview at your earliest convenience. Thank you.

Sincerely,

Simon Garfield

Enclosure

EDWARD WRIGHT
198 Flowerbed Drive
Ridgefield, New Jersey 16453
(609) 653-5423

August 15, 1997

Robert Bradley
President
Diversified Manufacturing, Inc.
1000 West End Trail
Milwaukee, WI 46633

Dear Mr. Bradley:

In 1990 I joined the management team of AlliedSignal's newly-formed Process Control Division. My goal was to build a Division-wide quality management, performance improvement and customer satisfaction organization, the best in the industry.

And, I have succeeded. The programs, processes and initiatives I led were critical to the organization's tremendous growth and expansion, from $95 million to $200+ million in annual revenues, from loss to strong profitability. Most significant were my contributions in:

- Leading the organization through ISO 9001 certification in record-breaking six months, positioning for strong and competitive international market expansion.
- Winning #1 customer satisfaction ratings within the industry.
- Achieving 100% on-time customer delivery.
- Changing the culture, vision and expectations of the organization.

Related achievements include millions of dollars in cost savings and avoidance through process redesign and 30% reduction in quality expense in core business units.

After years of success and achievement with AlliedSignal, I have decided to confidentially explore new professional opportunities. As such, I would welcome a personal interview to explore senior quality management positions with Diversified Manufacturing. I appreciate your time and will follow-up next week.

Sincerely,

Edward Wright

Enclosure

REAL ESTATE DEVELOPMENT
&
INVESTMENT

KeyWords, Action Verbs & High-Impact Phrases

To "Nail" Your Cover Letter:

* Joint Ventures & Partnerships

* Project Development & Construction Management

* Mixed-Use Commercial, Retail, Residential & Investment Properties

* Major Project Highlights

* Contract Negotiations

* Real Estate Workouts & Recovery

* Asset & Portfolio Management

* Regulatory & Government Affairs

* Environmental Management & Remediation

* ROI Analysis & Performance

JONATHAN P. SMITH
5032 Northern Peak
Carlsbad, California 98732
(619) 983-9222

DATE

President
Development Capital Corporation
1000 Rancho del Gato
Santa Fe, NM 87501

Dear Sir/Madam:

Throughout my 20-year Real Estate career, I have built and led successful development, investment finance, property management and brokerage/sales organizations. To each organization, I have provided the strategic, marketing, financial and operating expertise to deliver strong earnings and sustained revenue streams.

As President of MPR Equity, I built the corporation from concept into a well-established real estate investment group that has completed over $100 million in apartment and shopping center development projects. Most notable has been my success in identifying and negotiating innovative financing instruments with U.S., Canadian, German and Japanese investors, bankers and business partners. Further, I have consistently delivered projects on budget despite the "usual complications and crises."

My success in sales, marketing, leasing and asset maximization is equally strong and includes development of one of the largest and most profitable real estate brokerages in the Midwest.

As you review my resume, you will note that my experience has expanded beyond each corporation to include active leadership of county zoning and planning affairs, downtown economic revitalization initiatives, and both commercial and real estate banking. Now, at this point in my career, I am seeking new professional challenges and opportunities within the industry. Thus my interest in Development Capital Corporation and your search for a VP of Development.

Sincerely,

Jonathan P. Smith

Enclosure

PAUL E. COLLINS

10324 Mistletoe Lane   •   Baltimore, Maryland 21121   •   Phone (410) 599-2285

February 5, 1997

Stephen Mitchell
Managing Partner
Mitchell & Cohen Investments
4455 Oakwood Avenue
Cleveland, OH 44323

Dear Mr. Mitchell:

Recruited by Rieman Management Corporation (a diversified real estate investment and asset management group) in 1987, I was challenged to rebuild the property management function, accelerate leasing through innovative marketing efforts, and capture long-term cost savings to improve the net profitability of the portfolio.

Results were significant:

- 20%+ gain in net earnings with $5 million increase in gross possible income.
- 98.5% occupancy (highest in the company's portfolio of 25 properties).
- $500,000+ reduction in annual operating costs.
- 100% improvement in tenant service and satisfaction.

Concurrent with my financial gains, I orchestrated tremendous improvements in the operational capabilities, efficiency and productivity of an $80 million residential, commercial and recreational facility (one of the largest such properties in the country). Major projects included first-time automation and several system upgrades, improved preventive maintenance programs, enhanced service training for all employees, and full documentation of all operating policies and procedures.

The value I delivered to Rieman Management will sustain the portfolio for years to come. Now, however, I am seeking new professional challenges and opportunities where I can again provide strong and decisive property management and operating leadership.

I look forward to a personal interview for the position of Vice President of Investments and thank you in advance for your consideration. I prefer to discuss my compensation requirements at the time of our interview.

Sincerely,

Paul E. Collins

Enclosure

DANIEL R. POWELL
700 Lincoln Place
Baltimore, Maryland 21212

October 12, 1997

John Warner
President
Fidelity Capital Ventures
1000 Michigan Avenue
Washington, D.C. 22002

Dear Mr. Warner:

If you are active in real estate development, community development and/or large-scale, mixed-used construction projects, you will be interested in my qualifications.

- 20+ years' experience in real estate development and management in the U.S. and international markets.

- Complete development and management responsibility for over $500 million in projects over the past 10 years.

- Leadership of more than $450 million in project funding and public/private partnership financing programs.

Most significant, however, is my ability to drive projects through complex community, political and governmental channels. By providing a strong community vision and decisive action plan, I have won the support of community, political, business and financial leaders — support critical to project funding, development and profitable sale/leasing.

Please note that my expertise includes single and multifamily residential, commercial retail, commercial office, light industrial, health care facilities, technology centers, large-scale recreational facilities and more.

I would welcome the chance to explore potential opportunities with your investment firm and or any of your principal holdings, and appreciate your time in reviewing my qualifications. Thank you.

Sincerely,

Daniel R. Powell

Enclosure

SALES

KeyWords, Action Verbs & High-Impact Phrases

To "Nail" Your Cover Letter:

* Revenue Increases

* Profit Increases

* Market Share Increases

* New Product Launches

* Multi-Channel Distribution Development

* Global Expansion

* Sales Training & Team Leadership

* Key Account Successes

* Sales Force Automation

* Selling Cost Reductions

DENISE HARRIS

546 South 33rd Avenue
New York, New York 10011

Home (212) 645-2132
Office (212) 987-6000

October 21, 1997

John Brown
Vice President of Sales
Global Telecommunications
12900 Southside Avenue
San Bernardino, CA 98771

Dear Mr. Brown:

My strength lies in my ability to build customer partnerships and long-term sales relation-ships in a broad variety of industries and across diverse market segments. Working principally with CEOs, CFOs and other senior executives, I have built the rapport, established the trust and closed the sales that consistently outpaced competition.

In my current position, I have accelerated sales from moderate to top-level performance, consistently surpassing goals. In tandem, I have strengthened our account services to ensure we remain ahead of the competition within perhaps one of the toughest markets in the country. I am proud of my achievements, but anxious to secure a new sales position.

I would welcome the opportunity for a personal interview and can assure you that my drive, enthusiasm and professionalism will be of significant value in your sales efforts. Thank you.

Sincerely,

Denise Harris

Enclosure

MARGARET JOHNSTON
101 Wabash Avenue #983
Chicago, Illinois 60606
(847) 822-9603

June 24, 1997

Harger Howe & Associates, Inc.
Confidential Reply Service
50 Briar Hollow, Suite 320E-819
Houston, TX 77027

RE: Corporate Account Manager

Dear Sir/Madam:

As Director of Global OEM Sales for the past three years, I have planned and directed sales programs targeted to major multinational corporations worldwide. For the previous six years, I managed key account sales and business development programs in markets nationwide. Throughout all assignments, I have been challenged to build market presence, accelerate revenue growth and outperform competition. Results include:

- Increase in OEM sales from $19.5 million to $26 million within two years.

- Capture and/or expansion of more than 30 major accounts including AT&T/Lucent, Carrier, Digital, Ericsson, Nortel, Panasonic, Phillips, Sony, Xerox, Square D and Allen Bradley.

- Development of the Emerson account from initial penetration to more than $1.5 million in annual sales and recognition as Emerson's "Supplier of the Year."

- Strategic development and tactical implementation of complex selling programs targeted to key decision makers.

- Coordination of cross-functional account teams working cooperatively to penetrate, build and service key customer base.

My expertise lies in my ability to build customer relationships by responding to their specific technology and business requirements. In turn, I have consistently won major client contracts generating millions of dollars in revenues each year and thwarting potential competition. Further, I have excelled in the training, development, motivation and supervision of other top-producing sales executives.

Although secure in my current position, I am confidentially exploring new professional opportunities where I can continue to provide strong and decisive sales leadership. As such, I would welcome the chance to interview for the above-referenced position and thank you in advance for your consideration.

Sincerely,

Margaret Johnston

Enclosure

NICHOLAS HENDERSON

2343 Jefferson Boulevard
Arlington, Virginia 23068

Home (703) 642-4140
Office (703) 859-6991

April 4, 1997

Vice President of Human Resources
XYAN, Inc.
1012 West Ninth Avenue, Suite 100
King of Prussia, PA 19406

RE: Vice President, Sales & Marketing

Dear Sir/Madam:

As National Market Manager with AT&T, I bring to your organization 11 years of progressively responsible experience in the strategic planning, design and leadership of winning sales, marketing and business development programs. My expertise lies in my ability to research market demand, identify customer requirements, and deliver complete sales and support programs to both commercial and consumer markets. Notable achievements include:

- Design of two service-driven product extensions, including development of all marketing communications and full-scale market launch. **RESULT: $2 million in revenues within first year.**

- Creative concept and deployment of a series of promotional and marketing campaigns for the national introduction of a completely new product line. **RESULT: $3.5 million in monthly revenues within first year.**

- Realignment of pricing and market positioning strategies for AT&T's national account portfolio. **RESULT: Consistent wins over competition AND a measurable improvement in net profitability of each sales transaction.**

Complementing my ability to produce sales dollars are equally strong qualifications in training and leading professional sales teams, providing strategic market vision with appropriate tactical action plans, and responding to the constantly changing demands of the market. I lead by example and provide strong decision making, problem solving and project management skills.

If decisive and action-driven leadership are your goals, we should meet. At that time, I would be pleased to provide specific information regarding my salary history and current salary requirements. Be advised that I am currently employed and respect your confidentiality in my search. Thank you.

Sincerely,

Nicholas Henderson

Enclosure

KENNETH THOMPSON

503 Pembroke Lane   Home (415) 387-5424
San Francisco, California 99445   Office (415) 805-5740

July 2, 1997

Andrew Morrison
Morrison & Associates Executive Recruiters
425 East Main Street, Suite 12
San Francisco, CA 99446

Dear Mr. Morrison:

Increasing sales of data communications and data processing products is my expertise.

* As Director of Sales for Noonan, I have built a nationwide sales and marketing organization that in two years delivered revenues exceeding $5 million.

* As Vice President of Sales for Salaxi, I increased annual sales by 53%.

* As General Manager of National Accounts for DataTech, I directed the start-up of the corporation's MIS outsourcing organization and built a $15+ million annual revenue stream.

Throughout my management career, I have provided the strategic marketing and tactical sales leadership critical to the success of start-up, turnaround and high-growth technology corporations. My success is largely attributable to the combination of not only my sales expertise, but my years of training and experience in technology, engineering and systems.

My greatest strength lies in my ability to structure, negotiate and close complex sales transactions with key corporate accounts, OEMs, VARs and system integrators. I am equally effective in building and managing sales, technical service and support teams, and have extensive general management, P&L management and multi-site operating management experience.

If you are working with a client company seeking a well-qualified sales and marketing executive, I would welcome the opportunity to speak with you. Be advised that I prefer to remain in the San Francisco area and currently average over $150,000 in annual compensation.

Sincerely,

Kenneth Thompson

Enclosure

ANDREW KENNEDY
312 Saratoga Springs Road
Morrestown, New Jersey
Home (609) 289-5446   Office (609) 883-2680

November 15, 1997

James Malone
National Sales Manager
Burlington Industries
400 Friendly Avenue
Greensboro, NC 27421

Dear Mr. Malone:

I am writing to express my interest in professional sales, marketing and/or customer service opportunities with Burlington and have enclosed my resume for your review. Highlights of my career include:

- Five years of experience in sales, customer service and new business development.

- Strong qualifications in building and managing key account relationships (e.g., Johnson & Johnson, W.W. Grainger, Sterling Drug).

- Ability to identify and capitalize upon market opportunities to build revenues and strengthen customer relationships.

- Excellent technology skills with particular strengths in systems installation and customer/user training and support.

- Well-developed communication, interpersonal relations, project management and time management skills.

Most recently, I founded a small company to fund my college education. The company has grown from start-up to over $25,000 in first year revenues and won key account contracts. Although proud of my success, I am anxious to join the sales, marketing or customer service team of an established corporation. Thus my interest in Burlington and request for a personal interview.

Thank you.

Sincerely,

Andrew Kennedy

Enclosure

MICHAEL JENKINS

1281 Steel Street
Bethlehem, Pennsylvania 19068

Home (415) 642-4140
Office (415) 649-6991

DATE

Matthew Kinard
President
SAAB Motor Cars
1293 Century Avenue
Atlanta, GA 30129

Dear Mr. Kinard:

When I recently shopped for a new vehicle, I was at a crossroads. A car enthusiast my entire life, I vacillated between a Volvo and a Saab. Which offered the most for my money, which provided the best in service and which was most effectively merchandised? The answer was clear — it was the Volvo. Do you want to know why?

An accomplished sales executive (currently employed with Xytoc in Pittsburgh), I am perhaps more critical than most. When I decide to invest $20,000 ... $30,000 ... $40,000 in a product, I want to buy from an educated sales professional who understands my needs and my expectations. This was my experience with Volvo.

So ... what can Saab do to more effectively compete? We all know that it is more than just styling and presentation. It is the entire selling and customer management cycle. It is understanding the product and its value, and clearly translating that to each prospective customer through both direct and indirect channels. And this is where I believe I can be of significant value to the Saab sales organization.

Do not misinterpret my intentions. I am not a car salesman and never have any intentions of pursuing that career path. I am, however, a talented, aggressive and determined sales executive who understands the dynamics of selling, product management, merchandising and customer loyalty. It is this expertise I wish to bring to Saab and through which I guarantee to deliver results.

I would welcome the chance to meet with you to explore senior-level sales and market management opportunities with Saab, and share my personal experience as an "on-the-street" consumer. I'm sure you'll be surprised by my feedback and encouraged by my recommendations.

Sincerely,

Michael Jenkins

Enclosure

ADAM F. EDMONDS
418 Alexander Avenue
San Jacquim, California 94546
(654) 376-7925

March 10, 1997

Michael Winston
President
Bendix Corporation
1809 South Plains Avenue
Denver, CO 32332

Dear Mr. Winston:

Success. It is the ability to translate the strategic marketing plan into tactical sales action, driving revenue growth, improving earnings and outperforming the competition.

This is the value I bring to your organization. As **Vice President of Sales & Marketing, National Sales Manager** and **Sales & Marketing Director** with several advanced technology companies, I led my teams to unprecedented market performance:

- Growth from $250,000 to $7 million in sales over two years for my most recent employer.
- Revitalization and return to profitability of Intel, Inc., with a 40% gain in sales revenues and 35% improvement in profitability.
- Capture of the first revenue increase in over seven years for Miller's Telecommunications Group.
- Leadership of high-profile sales and marketing programs throughout Europe, Latin America, Far East and the entire Pacific Rim for MRT Systems.

These achievements represent the quality and caliber of my entire professional career — identify and capture new market opportunities, build and develop top-producing field sales teams, and spearhead new product innovations.

My goal is a senior-level sales and marketing leadership position with a company poised for strong and aggressive growth. I guarantee that the strength of my market experience, product knowledge, leadership competencies and personal selling talents will be of significant value. Thank you and I look forward to speaking with you.

Sincerely,

Adam F. Edmonds

Enclosure

202

DARRELL ALBERTSON
1305 West Swamp Creek Road
Troutville, Louisiana 70525

Home (541) 854-9075   DALBERT@aol.com   Fax (541) 854-6694

February 14, 1997

Rebecca Covington
Managing Partner
Westwood Advertising
800 Regency Boulevard
West Hollywood, CA 90058

Dear Ms. Covington:

As a well-qualified Sales & Marketing Professional, I am writing in anticipation that you may be interested in a candidate with:

- Nine years of increasingly responsible experience in sales, new business development, client/ customer service, public relations and <u>revenue growth</u>.

- Extensive background in advertising, media and press relations with particular success in guiding clients in the <u>development of winning advertising, marketing and promotional campaigns</u>.

- Expertise in building and maintaining <u>profitable client relationships</u> against market competition.

- Management of clients' complete <u>advertising, marketing, public relations and government affairs programs</u>.

- Combination of <u>strong creative design, copyrighting and production skills</u>.

My goal is a field sales or sales management position where I can utilize the combination of my personal selling skills with my creative talents and unique abilities to design and deliver high-impact, multimedia ad campaigns.

I look forward to meeting with you. Thank you.

Sincerely,

Darrell Albertson

Enclosure

ELIZABETH R. WERNER
21 East Washington Parkway
Detroit, Michigan 48995
(619) 232-6544

March 16, 1997

John Heritage
President
Data Tech Corporation
1900 Avenue of the Americas, 19th Floor
New York, NY 10011

Dear Mr. Heritage:

Building long-term client relationships is my expertise. Throughout my 20-year Sales & Marketing career, I have designed and implemented the strategies, plans and actions that have consistently delivered strong and sustainable revenue and profit growth. Some achievements that may be of particular note include:

- Start-up to $4.5 million in annual revenues for Greener's Service Industries business unit. Closed both national and international customer agreements.

- Successful turnaround of Greener's Corporate Accounts division from loss to profitability within 20 months through the development of new pricing strategies and revitalization of product mix.

- Development and launch of more than 16 solutions-based products to meet the specific needs of a diverse clientele. Instrumental in positioning Johnson Systems as the #1 provider of commercial products throughout the U.S.

These achievements are indicative of the quality and caliber of my entire professional career — identify and capitalize upon emerging market opportunities, provide market-driven products, and nurture client relationships to ensure their trust and commitment far into the future. In addition, I have also created top-flight sales training programs to train field sales teams in strategic selling, client relationship management and contract negotiations.

My goal is a senior-level sales management position with an organization poised for growth. I would welcome a personal interview to further discuss your current needs for strong and decisive sales leadership and appreciate your time and consideration.

Sincerely,

Elizabeth R. Werner

Enclosure

Jeffrey A. Steele

4325 South River Road
Knoxville, Tennessee 37291

Home (423) 392-6837   Office (423) 557-4774

June 1, 1997

Charles Jamison
Vice President of Corporate Sales
American Express
1000 Express Way
Wichita, KS 60221

Dear Mr. Jamison:

Building market value is my expertise. Whether challenged to launch a start-up venture, facilitate revenue growth within established business markets, or accelerate expansion for a high-growth business unit, I have consistently delivered strong financial results throughout my tenure with PRG Bancorp. Most notably:

- As a member of the nationwide launch team for the Corporate Card Division, built region from start-up to $50 million in annualized charge volume with 22 new accounts.

- As Regional Sales Manager for the Travel Management Services Division, delivered 25%+ growth in revenues and profits within a well-established business unit.

- As Director of National Accounts for the Establishment Services Division, guided organization through a period of accelerated growth with $800+ million increase in annual volume.

Through my efforts in customer management, new product launch, new market development and regional/national sales management, I delivered strong results and consistently outperformed the competition.

Now, at this juncture in my career, I am exploring new professional challenges in sales and marketing management. Thus my interest in meeting with you to discuss management opportunities with American Express, and the value, leadership and performance results I bring to your organization.

I appreciate your consideration and look forward to speaking with you.

Sincerely,

Jeffrey A. Steele

Enclosure

SENIOR MANAGEMENT

KeyWords, Action Verbs & High-Impact Phrases

To "Nail" Your Cover Letter:

* Strategic Planning, Vision & Direction

* Domestic & International Business

* Start-Up, Turnaround & High-Growth Companies

* Revenue & Profit Growth

* New Product, Service & Technology Development

* Corporate Culture Change

* IPOs, Joint Ventures, Alliances & Partnerships

* Cross-Functional Team Building & Leadership

* Tactical Planning & Operations Management

* Productivity, Efficiency & Quality Improvement

RICHARD F. SMITH
1290 South Plains Avenue
Kansas City, Kansas 66213
(913) 239-5539

February 3, 1997

Matthew Brooks
President & CEO
Permatec, Inc.
19002 Southside Boulevard
Sherman Oaks, CA 98774

Dear Matt:

After much thought and deliberation, I've made the decision to leave my current position as President of CD Laboratories. It was a difficult decision, but appropriate for both personal and professional reasons.

With the organization since 1989, I joined as Operations Manager, was promoted to Director of Marketing in 1990 and to President in 1995. Results have been significant and include revenue growth of more than 150%, with more than $1 million from development of contract manufacturing with business partners worldwide.

Previously, during my seven-year tenure with Russell-Towne, I spearheaded successful product development, sales and marketing programs worldwide, capturing over $200 million in new revenues.

My current goal is a senior-level operating, sales and/or marketing management position with an organization poised for long-term growth and expansion. And I need your help in identifying that opportunity.

If you are aware of an organization seeking strong, decisive and market-driven leadership, I would appreciate the referral and a direct recommendation, if possible. You've seen firsthand what I can do, the challenges I have met and the results I have delivered. Now, I need a new company, new challenges and new opportunities. I would also consider, as appropriate, a potential acquisition

I look forward to speaking with you. If it would be more convenient to contact me during the day, you can reach me at (913) 222-5311, in confidence. If, in the future, there are any doors I can open for you, please do not hesitate to contact me. Thank you.

Sincerely,

Richard F. Smith

Enclosure

STEVEN JONES

500 West Barstow #102
Fresno, California   93407

Phone   (209) 666-7449
Fax   (209) 665-4450

March 3, 1997

Ivan Lewis
The Germany Group
1900 West Park Avenue, 3rd Floor
New York, NY 10010

Dear Mr. Lewis:

It's not often that one has the opportunity to combine years of corporate marketing, sales and general management experience into an entrepreneurial venture. I've had the opportunity to do it twice - first as a Minority Owner and Board Member of The MBR Company and more recently as Majority Owner of Diemectec, Inc.

In retrospect, I can fully appreciate the strength and value of my corporate background. Advancing through the management ranks with General Foods, Coca-Cola and Pepsi, I acquired tremendous experience in strategic planning, marketing, business development, operating management and more.

Once faced with the new challenges of start-up and emerging growth ventures, I was able to apply that knowledge and experience. In turn, both of these organizations have prospered under not only my board leadership but also my hands-on operating management.

In addition, I bring to your firm experience in capital raising, investor road show presentations, financing and business development. Most notably, I have recently executed a successful merger, bringing both organizations together, merging the cultures, eliminating the redundancy and expanding the market penetration.

Currently, I am exploring new challenges and opportunities either as an investor and/or operating executive. The ideal situation would require both strategic and operating leadership of a new venture, turnaround or high-growth organization.

I look forward to exploring opportunities and appreciate your time in reviewing my qualifications.

Sincerely,

Steven Jones

Enclosure

Route 7 Box 350
Allentown, Pennsylvania 17571
Home (717) 781-7257   Fax (717) 781-5731

May 15, 1997

Samuel Spencer
Chairman
Total Energy, Inc.
23 Cumberland Highway
Portland, OR 41214

Dear Mr. Spencer:

What value do I bring to Total Energy? The answers are clearcut:

* 18 years of strong leadership experience as **President/COO, Managing Director** and **Vice President of Marketing & Business Development.**
* Broad-based experience across diverse product, service and technology industries.
* Success in merging the strategic with the tactical, delivering long-term gains in revenues and profits, outpacing the competition and dominating the marketplace.

To each organization, I have provided strong leadership with measurable results:

* **100% revenue growth** as CEO of Bridle Incorporated.
* **30% growth in market share** and **20% profit increase** as Vice President with Morrisman Industries.
* **25% growth in national distribution** as Vice President with Pacific Green Industries.
* Three amazing "bottom-line" turnaround and business restructuring initiatives.

Characterized by others as visionary, decisive and charismatic, I possess keen instincts and strategies to quickly effect change and improvement. My management style is participative, high-energy, results-driven and "hands-on". Further, my technical qualifications in both manufacturing automation and PC/MIS technology are strong.

Although active in my consulting practice, I am interested in a unique opportunity to return to a larger organization with a solid business infrastructure and a recognizable need for strong and decisive leadership. I look forward to pursuing such opportunities with Total Energy and thank you for your consideration. A resume will follow as per your request.

Sincerely,

Dennis Jamison

GERALD FAYGEN

125 Fourth Avenue West, Apt. 12
San Francisco, California 91382
Home (714) 793-2892   Office (714) 573-5968

September 1, 1997

Murray Morestein
Chairman
Crextar, Inc.
1900 Wilshire Boulevard, #12
Los Angeles, CA 98222

Dear Mr. Morestein:

Success. I believe it lies in one's ability to merge the strategic with the tactical, to understand the market and competition, to control the finances, and to build a strong and decisive management team. No one function can be accountable for performance. It is the interconnection of everything and the combined strength of the management team.

Success and improved corporate value is what I have delivered throughout my career. Note the following contributions:

- Growth of X-Lab Company from $250 million to $6 billion in assets.

- Successful operating turnaround of the organization with overall profit improvement of more than 90%.

- Development and nationwide market launch of a new family of mutual funds, now a $3 billion asset base.

- Introduction of customer-driven services, programs and management teams to gain market lead and outpace the competition.

Most notable has been my success across diverse functional lines — from corporate-level strategic planning and product development to "hands-on" management of IS, staffing and process redesign initiatives. I lead by example, expect consistently strong performance from my teams, and in turn, have delivered strong and sustainable financial results.

Now, I'm ready for a new challenge and new opportunity. Thus my interest in meeting with you to explore your need for senior-level operating management talent.

Sincerely,

Gerald Faygen

Enclosure

210

CHRISTOPHER FRANKLIN
259 Court Street
Greenwich, Connecticut 06495
Home (203) 738-8704   Office (202) 789-7548

March 10, 1997

Anthony Arnold
President & CEO
Top Cat Apparel
2888 Island View
Garden City, NY 11542

Dear Mr. Arnold:

High-growth companies require leadership talent that is broad in perspective, merging all core functional disciplines to achieve common goals and deliver aggressive performance results.

In my career, I have done just that. With more than 15 years of senior-level management experience, I personally directed virtually all operating, strategic, marketing and financial functions. Most significantly, I delivered strong performance in earnings, cost reduction, process improvement and long-range business development.

High-growth companies also require visionary leadership. It is not enough to manage the day-to-day operations. Rather, it is critical that the leadership team provide direction, action and success.

My achievements clearly reflect my ability to deliver:

- In my current turnaround general management assignment, I am creating and implementing strategic and tactical plans to build revenues by 10%-15% over the next year.

- Previously, as General Manager of Accounting and IS organizations, I captured over $13 million in cost reductions, implemented advanced technology and improved quality ratings to above 97%.

- In my entrepreneurial venture, I transitioned a concept into a fully-operational business, negotiated seed financing and achieved profitability in first year.

Perhaps most significant, high-growth companies demand excellence and require leadership able to strengthen the value of the corporation, its products, its technology and its customer service. Again, I have excelled.

Currently, I am involved in an interim management situation and am exploring new career challenges. Thus my interest in meeting with you to explore such opportunities where I can provide aggressive and decisive leadership, action and results. I look forward to your call.

Sincerely,

Christopher Franklin

Enclosure

LAWRENCE SWANSON

38 Desert Road
Phoenix, Arizona 78481

LarryS@aol.com   Phone: (602) 313-0208

October 2, 1997

Lester Lobdell
President
Maddox, Inc.
1900 Wabash Avenue, Suite 120
Chicago, IL 60842

Dear Mr. Lobdell:

At age 34, I've risen through the ranks of several large corporations, starting with a career in Engineering and Technology, transitioning into Finance and, most recently, focusing on Marketing and International Business Development. The sum of these experiences has now prepared me for a position in General Management where I can integrate these functions and provide strong and decisive leadership.

* As a Marketing & Business Development Manager, I am currently spearheading United's aggressive entry into emerging Southeast Asian markets and creating innovative manufacturing and marketing alliances.

* As a Financial Professional, I provided high-level planning and analytical support to United and several of their operating subsidiaries to facilitate reengineering and organizational change initiatives.

* As an Engineering Professional, I was promoted to a leadership position within one year and directed several sophisticated technology development and implementation projects.

Equally strong are my planning, organizational, problem solving and communication skills. I thrive in fast-paced, technologically-sophisticated environments that require innovative leadership and decisive action. Now, I am ready to meet new challenges and deliver strong results.

I would welcome a personal interview at your earliest convenience and appreciate your time and assistance.

Sincerely,

Lawrence Swanson

Enclosure

212

Kyle Lawson

500 Oakmont Court
St. Louis, Missouri 60021
(314) 261-8123

July 23, 1997

George C. Henry
President
Airmetric Corporation
12100 72nd Avenue Southwest
Seattle, WA 98112

Dear Mr. Henry:

I was recruited to Data Masters Corporation in 1987. Revenues were only $12 million, but the company had strong technical competencies and a real vision for its market. Through my efforts and those of my colleagues, we have built Data Masters into a $50 million public company with market presence worldwide. Most notably, my contributions include:

- Provided strategic, financial, tactical and operating leadership of several critical mergers, acquisitions and partnership programs.

- Championed the acquisition and development of more than $15 million in information and telecommunications technology resources to build an interactive, multiplexed global technology network supporting 30,000+ users worldwide.

- Enhanced profitability through efforts in organizational development, employee development, team building, quality and performance improvement.

- Created and led the North American sales organization, tripling sales in the company's strategic product line within just three years.

My tenure at Data Masters has been strong and my contributions have been a true catalyst for their success. Now, however, I am seeking new professional challenges and new opportunities where I can continue to provide decisive operating, technology, business development, sales and organizational leadership.

I would welcome a personal interview to explore senior operating management positions with Airmetric Corporation, and appreciate both your time and consideration. Thank you.

Sincerely,

Kyle Lawson

Enclosure

PATRICK WILLIAMSON
31654 South 27th Street
Las Cruces, New Mexico 78551

Residence (502) 612-3424

Business (502) 997-7311

January 10, 1997

John Ramsett
The Ramsett Group
2500 Braxton Road #1002
Austin, TX 79551

Dear Mr. Ramsett:

With several of Syntex Corporation's largest operating companies, I have progressed through increasingly responsible finance, operating and general management positions. To each, I have provided strategic and tactical leadership:

- Syntex Wireless Terminals Division — Currently orchestrating start-up of new venture delivering PCS services with GSM and CDMA technologies.

- Syntex Communications — Successfully spearheaded massive corporate culture change, 350% gain in organizational productivity and 40% headcount reduction.

- Syntex/Microbyte Systems — Member of 12-person senior management team leading successful reorganization and return to profitability.

- Microbyte Information Systems — Guided venture start-up and fast-track growth of organization to over $70 million in annual revenues.

With cross-functional experience in Strategic Planning, Finance, Information Systems, Administration and Multi-Site Operations, I offer a strong portfolio of qualifications and results. My management style is direct and decisive, yet flexible in responding to constantly changing organizational, finance and market demands.

If you are working with a client company in need of strong, direct and decisive senior-level general and/or financial management, I would welcome the chance to explore the opportunity. Please be advised that I am open to relocation and that my compensation has averaged $150,000+ over the past several years. Thank you.

Sincerely,

Patrick Williamson

Enclosure

214

NEWMAN GRANT
9344 River Bend
Charleston, West Virginia 32145
(304) 354-6541

November 1, 1997

Leon Dische
DRG Partners, Inc.
235 Cross Point Road
Katonah, NY 15161

Dear Mr. Dische:

I've had a great career! A career that has spanned diverse industries — from leading edge environmental technologies and services to marine products manufacturing. Most people, however, are interested in my experiences with both Grayson Music and Grayson Video. Joining the former in 1991, I was challenged to reengineer and revitalize a large manufacturing operation. Results were impressive and included:

* 260% increase in annual sales revenues, 600% gain in international sales and 220% increase in operations productivity.
* Negotiation of innovative alliances with Harley Davidson, Hard Rock, Elvis Presley Enterprises and other corporate partners.

Based upon my performance, I was promoted and transferred to Grayson Video. My challenge was to accelerate corporate growth through new market development, new product development, acquisitions and international expansion. Again, results were impressive with up to 45% growth annually.

A "General Manager" by trade, I have held a series of high-level positions including four years as President/CEO, two years as General Manager and three years as EVP/Board Director. The value I have delivered to each organization can be measured by growth in revenue and earnings, success in cost reduction and performance improvement, and achievement in positioning each against tough competition.

The value I bring to DRG Partners is the diversity of my experience — diversity in industries, markets, products, technologies and business disciplines. I enjoy the challenges of start-up, turnaround and high-growth organizations, and have provided the strength in strategic, tactics and leadership to consistently improve results.

Now, I'm ready for new challenges and new opportunities, and would welcome the chance to interview as DRG's CEO. I am now working on a long-term consulting assignment and am being aggressively recruited for a permanent executive position with the organization. However, I am confidentially exploring other opportunities and look forward to speaking with you.

Sincerely,

Newman Grant

Enclosure

GEORGE RICHARDSON
1007 Mountain View Road
Charlotte, North Carolina 27710

Home: 919-783-4922

Office: 919-797-9100

March 15, 1997

Yvonne McMasters
President
Overhead Manufacturing
1900 Parker Road
Syracuse, NY 11441

Dear Ms. McMasters:

My skill set is quite unique. I'm an Attorney, CPA and most importantly, Senior Executive, successful in combining core business functions to provide strong, decisive and profitable leadership. The scope of my experience is broad, spanning countless industries worldwide. Most notable is my success in corporate development, M&A transactions, corporate finance/recapitalization and international trade. Highlights are included on the enclosed resume.

My operations, transactions and projects have impacted major companies worldwide — Metromedia, Mitsubishi, Bank of America, GATX, Howard Hughes Medical Institute, Pennzoil, PaineWebber, AEA Investors and others. In turn, I bring to your organization the wealth of experience I have gained through these efforts and a demonstrated record of financial and operating achievement.

Currently, I am exploring unique and dynamic executive opportunities where I can continue to provide integrated operating, legal and financial leadership. Your firm was personally recommended and, as such, I am enclosing a resume for your review. I look forward to hearing from you and do appreciate your time.

Sincerely,

George Richardson

Enclosure

DANIEL WARNER

329 Prairie Wind Trail
Omaha, Nebraska 32466

Office (642) 379-1034   Fax (642) 376-2691

April 9, 1997

Greg Parker
Managing Partner
New Media Entertainment
1090 Wilshire Boulevard, #212
Los Angeles, CA 90022

Dear Mr. Parker:

Throughout the past several years, I have worked closely with Disney, Time Warner, Mattel, Eastman Kodak and others in the introduction of pioneering digital technology and their specific applications to the film, video and multimedia broadcast industries. The experience has been extraordinary and provided me with the opportunity to work closely with teams of talented designers, animators and technology programmers.

With a unique blend of senior management talents in general business, operations, sales and marketing, I have consistently delivered strong financial results in challenging start-up, turnaround and high-growth organizations. Through a combined emphasis on new business development, new products and the redesign/improvement of core business functions, I have consistently surpassed performance objectives and returned strong and sustainable results.

Just as significant is my strength in negotiations — building and maintaining relationships with top-level decision makers to drive forward special projects, new technologies and market expansion. I pride myself on my ability to identify and capture emerging market opportunities to build value, outperform competition and drive strong revenue growth.

Most recently, I have negotiated the sale of Oasis, Inc. to a private investor group and am now exploring the opportunity to transition my skills and experience into a senior-level position within the entertainment industry. My goal is a top-flight position with an entertainment company committed to the development of leading edge technologies and aggressive in market development/positioning.

I look forward to speaking with you and can assure you that the strength of my management, marketing and technology skills will be of significant value in your current and long-term business ventures. Thank you.

Sincerely,

Daniel Warner

Enclosure

THOMAS ANDERSON

3642 Vine Street
Sacramento, California 98314

Residence   (661) 930-0714
Business   (661) 964-1414

June 1, 1997

Collin Price
President
B&G Chemical Corporation
12900 Mountain View Plaza, #211
Colorado Springs, CO 77441

Dear Mr. Price:

An organization is only equal to the value, strength and commitment of its workforce. This is the underlying foundation for Mastem Corporation, the organization which I have built and profitably managed for more than 15 years.

Beginning with the company while still completing my undergraduate degree, I advanced rapidly and have held full P&L responsibility since 1980. Today, as CEO, I lead the entire organization, its nationwide public relations efforts and its long-term development and further expansion.

The revenue and profit growth of Mastem have been significant, and we have established a strong foothold against Prentice Hall and other large competitors. Without decreasing the tremendous value of our sales, service and marketing efforts, it is important to note that our greatest asset is our workforce — a team of 110 individuals, each of whom is committed to our growth, prosperity and success.

By creating an environment that promotes and rewards excellence, I have fostered the growth of the company. By designing innovative employee empowerment and recognition programs, I have improved retention and built a team that is recognized throughout the community for their work and non-work related projects.

Now, at this juncture in my career, I am seeking new executive challenges and opportunities where I can continue to provide strong, decisive and effective operating leadership. Thus my interest in B&G Chemical and request for a personal interview.

Sincerely,

Thomas Anderson

Enclosure

DAVID GROSSMAN
9354 South 94th Avenue
St. Louis, Missouri 63184
(666) 674-4262

October 17, 1997

James Lexington
Independence Technology, Inc.
1900 Paul Revere, Suite 122
Boston, MA 04131

Dear Mr. Lexington:

Here are the facts:

- Twelve years of senior-level operating management experience (President, CEO, Corporate Vice President) within the emerging technology industries worldwide.

- Extensive P&L management experience with full organizational control of strategic planning, market planning, R&D, technology development, human resources, corporate development, business process redesign, budgeting, organizational development and a host of other general management functions.

- Leadership of successful international joint ventures, technology transfers, technology commercialization projects, strategic alliances, IPOs and related corporate development initiatives.

- Advanced knowledge of software, telecommunications, information processing, networking, digital electronic, systems integration and electronic photographic technologies.

- Expertise in start-up ventures, turnaround business units and high-growth corporations.

- Strong and sustainable revenue and profit gains. Equally impressive cost reductions, quality gains and improvements in performance/productivity.

My goal is a top-level operating management position with a high-tech company in need of strong, decisive and market-driven leadership. My compensation requirements are flexible and I am open to relocation for the right opportunity.

I look forward to speaking with you and appreciate your efforts.

Sincerely,

David Grossman

219

JEFFERSON COLLINS
9040 Overland Pass
Portland, Oregon 96110
Home (741) 472-5029   Office (741) 437-7369

April 10, 1997

Harold Westin
President
Northwest Environmental
19200 East 23rd Avenue South
Kirkland, WA 98741

Dear Mr. Westin:

- Between 1992 and 1995, I led the successful turnaround of Diabolique, Inc., delivering a 250%+ improvement in net profit and 50%+ gain in annual revenues (40% of which were generated from new products/new markets).

- Between 1988 to 1991, with full P&L responsibility for a Cramer's business unit, I reduced costs by $2 million and drove revenue growth of 40% to $250 million with a 30% increase in gross profitability.

- Between 1987 and 1988, I reengineered two of Gibraltar's business units, successfully developed four new products and launched a $2 million manufacturing venture.

These achievements are indicative of the strength and diversity of my career. Working as the #1/#2 operating executive of growth, turnaround and mature businesses ($20 million to $250 million in annual revenues) has allowed me to demonstrate my flexibility, my strengths in problem solving and leadership, and success in decision making for action and results.

Currently, I am pursuing new management opportunities where I can continue to drive domestic and/or international market growth while providing strong "hands-on" P&L operating leadership. As such, I look forward to speaking with you to pursue such opportunities and thank you for your time and consideration in reviewing my qualifications.

Please contact me at your earliest convenience. Be assured that I will deliver results.

Sincerely,

Jefferson Collins

Enclosure

PETER CAVANAUGH
2323 Kennedy Street
Arlington, Texas 57744
Email: PCV@net.com
(701) 644-9854

May 2, 1997

Nicholas Rhone
Frontier Equity
9845 Commercial Towers, Suite 211
Fairfax, VA 23774

Dear Mr. Rhone:

I am writing to explore your need for a President / CEO / COO of one of your portfolio companies. With more than 20 years of top-flight executive management and leadership experience, I have met the challenges of new ventures, turnaround businesses and high-growth expansion ($20 million to $250 million in annual revenues). To each, I have delivered strong and sustainable operating results:

* 250%+ improvement in net profitability and 50%+ revenue growth for Armatech, Inc. (40% generated from new product/new market development).

* 30% increase in gross profitability and $2 million operating cost reduction for Jollers, Inc.

* Negotiation of $2 million manufacturing venture and $2 million acquisition to accelerate Chrisstel's growth within the industrial engineered materials market.

My strengths include identifying and developing new business opportunities, restructuring and strengthening existing operations, introducing advanced technologies and accelerating new product development/launch. I am decisive in my leadership style, yet flexible in responding to constantly changing market, economic and business demands. Most significant has been my success in structuring complex transactions to facilitate market growth, improved earnings and long-range corporate development. Further, each business under my leadership has experienced accelerated and sustained revenue and profit growth.

I would welcome the opportunity to speak with you at your earliest convenience. Thank you for your consideration.

Sincerely,

Peter Cavanaugh

Enclosure

221

JOHN WELLINGTON
87544 Spring Garden
Placentia, California 98551
(311) 888-8841

July 23, 1997

Alexander Larness
President & CEO
IO-Lab Technologies
1200 Washington Way
Menlo Park, CA 98441

Dear Mr. Larness:

I am a successful entrepreneur who has developed, financed and built eight new ventures through-out my career. Combined revenues have exceeded $35 million annually with my current project forecasted to generate $45 million in first year sales. The diversity of my industry experience ranges from private tennis and racquetball clubs to state-of-the-art technologies.

So ... why do I want a job?

I'm looking for stability and a change in life-style. The years of entrepreneurial ventures have been both personally and professionally rewarding. However, the toll on myself and my family has been significant. Now, at age 45, I am interested in channeling my skills in a new direction where I can provide senior operating support to an established, turnaround and/or high-growth corporation.

The wealth of experience I bring to an organization is vast with particular emphasis on strategic planning, product development, marketing, financing and investment solicitation. Just as significant are my strengths in operating management, including staffing, sales, customer service, pricing, account-ing/financial reporting, purchasing and long-range development.

If you are seeking an individual who can make an immediate and positive impact upon your operations, revenue stream and profit margins, we should talk. I desire a position in a dynamic environment that offers flexibility, challenge and opportunity.

Sincerely,

John Wellington

Enclosure

PAUL MEDPATH

953 South Ridgefield Avenue
Bloomfield Hills, Michigan 48304
(810) 554-3221

January 10, 1997

Norman Schwartz
President
Peabody Holdings, Inc.
1200 Parkside Avenue
Ft. Lauderdale, FL 33221

Dear Norm:

It's been a while since you and I have had the opportunity to talk. I hope that the New Year has started off on a positive note and that you look forward to a prosperous 1997.

Currently, M&M/Mars Enterprises is launching a corporate-wide reorganization. Although I feel confident in my career track with the company, I also think that it is appropriate to investigate new professional challenges and opportunities where I can continue to provide strong and decisive financial leadership. As such, if you are aware of an organization seeking a candidate with my qualifications, I would certainly appreciate the recommendation and/ or contact information.

I have enclosed a copy of my resume for review. To briefly summarize my 10-year career with M&M/Mars, please note the following results:

* Return to profitability of the $1 billion Midwest business unit with a $40 million increase in volume and profits.
* Capture of more than $30 million in operating costs through redesign of the company's nationwide finance organization.
* Introduction of leading edge information, communication and EDI technologies.
* Creation of a proactive finance function, positioned as a strategic and tactical business partner to operating units nationwide.

I appreciate your assistance and your confidentiality. If there is anything that I can do in return, please do not hesitate to call. Thank you.

Sincerely,

Paul Medpath

Enclosure

WENDELL WOODS
9821 Ranchers Way
Richardson, Texas 65547
(654) 484-5445

June 5, 1997

Carson Dillard
President - Domestic Operations
RJR Nabisco
1910 5th Avenue
New York, NY 10010

Dear Mr. Dillard:

Building corporate value is my expertise — value that is measured in increased revenues, improved earnings, reduced operating costs, and more competitive and sustainable market advantages. It is this expertise, along with strong strategic planning, financial, M&A and operating management skills, that I bring to the position of Chief Operating Officer.

As a Vice President, Director and Senior Business Manager with Coca-Cola, Quaker and General Foods, I have guided CEOs, CFOs and other top executives through the complex challenges associated with global expansion, LBO and IPO transactions, product line rationalizations, new venture start-ups, business unit divestitures and more. To each, I have provided the strategic and tactical leadership critical to meeting our financial, operating and market objectives. Most notably, I:

* Expanded General Food's resource pool by $400 million, part of the company's massive reengineering and global market repositioning effort.
* Revitalized dormant business units and reenergized Quaker's entire strategic planning function.
* Advanced rapidly during my tenure with Coke's, captured $200 million in savings and negotiated one of the largest contracts in the company's history.

Now, at this juncture in my career, I am seeking the opportunity to transition my qualifications into a high-growth corporation in need of strong and decisive executive leadership. Thus my interest in your organization and request for a personal interview. Thank you.

Sincerely,

Wendell Woods

Enclosure

ROBERT JACKSON
432 Jefferson Avenue
Montgomery, Alabama 86577

Phone (647) 475-8438

Fax (647) 475-2380

December 3, 1997

Charles Singleton
Singleton International Search Partners
100 Peach Tree Lane
Atlanta, GA 40440

Dear Mr. Singleton:

I have had a very successful career as the President, CEO, COO and Vice President of several corporations — two of which I have owned. To each start-up, turnaround and high-growth venture, I have provided both the strategic and tactical leadership for significant financial gain.

Now, however, I want a "good job." Although I may be interested in a #1 spot with a small organization, I am most interested in an exciting and growth-driven opportunity where I can provide corporate development, marketing and/or operating leadership. At age 41, it's time to enjoy my career.

The breadth of my experience is quite extensive and includes:

*   Full P&L and operating management responsibility for corporations, subsidiaries, divisions, joint ventures and partnerships worldwide.
*   Leadership of countless product development, commercialization and market launch programs.
*   Aggressive control of accelerating operating, marketing and overhead costs with consistent improvements in net profit contributions.
*   Negotiation of successful investment financing agreements to fund IPOs, acquisitions and other corporate development programs.
*   Extensive business experience throughout North America, Europe and the Pacific Rim.

Please note that my experience includes both entrepreneurial start-up ventures as well as more mature and larger corporations. While employed with Serpent, I progressed rapidly through the "traditional career ladder" in a more structured corporate environment.

I would welcome the chance to explore any current search assignments you feel are appropriate for an individual with my qualifications. Be advised that I am open to relocation and my salary requirements are negotiable.

Sincerely,

Robert Jackson

Enclosure

225

LARRY BLOOMFIELD

12 Gator Road
Boca Raton, Florida 33486
Fax (407) 541-7783

Home (407) 541-2514

Office (305) 985-1005

August 1, 1997

Philip Newfield
PNC Investments
342 The Marsh
Hilton Head, SC 64774

Dear Mr. Newfield:

In 1983 I had an idea for a new business venture. Thirteen years later, that idea has been transformed into a $6+ million corporation with 24 operating locations throughout the Miami metro region. Growth has been steady and progressive; earnings consistently stronger year after year.

My role as President has included all operating functions of the entire organization — strategic planning, sales, marketing, purchasing, distribution, human resources, PC technology and corporate finance/accounting. I am particularly strong in the areas of real estate leasing and legal affairs, and have personally managed complex contracts, agreements and corporate law transactions.

Based upon my achievements, I was featured in the September 1995 edition of *Forbes Magazine*, citing my expertise in market development, business management and profitability. Now, however, I have decided to sell the corporation and am interested in senior-level operating management position where I can provide strong, decisive and effective leadership.

If you are seeking a candidate with my qualifications, experience and track record, I would welcome a personal interview. Thank you for taking the time to review my qualifications.

Sincerely,

Larry Bloomfield

SERVICE ORGANIZATION MANAGEMENT

KeyWords, Action Verbs & High-Impact Phrases

To "Nail" Your Cover Letter:

* Workflow Process Design & Implementation

* Quality, Efficiency & Productivity Management

* Customer Service, Satisfaction & Retention

* Field Service Management

* Order Entry & Fulfillment

* Personnel Training & Team Building

* Cost Reduction & Avoidance

* New Product & Service Launch

* Revenue & Profit Generation

* Operations Consolidation & Integration

HELEN P. GARRETT

200 Hillside Drive
Silver Spring, Maryland 20660
Email: HPG@AOL.COM

Home: (301) 536-5408

Office: (301) 998-0770

February 25, 1997

Donald P. Torrance
President
General Foods Corporation
3943 Ivy Hills
St. Paul, MN 55441

Dear Mr. Torrance:

To win a competitive lead in the marketplace today requires innovation and expertise in service, support and operations. This is the value I bring to General Foods. With more than 15 years of senior-level operating management experience, I have delivered strong and sustainable financial performance:

- 40% volume growth for my current employer with significant reduction in operating costs.
- $400 million in cost avoidance and savings for Keller's Nationwide Operations.
- 15% annual business growth in Keller's Systems Integration Business.

The scope of my management responsibility is broad and includes strategic planning, marketing, multi-site operations, service delivery, sales, customer management, contracts, facilities, technology and human resources. Most significant, however, is my ability to build relationships across diverse market and customer sectors, outpacing the competition and improving customer loyalty.

Now, at this point in my professional career, I am interested in exploring new senior-level operating management opportunities within the services industry and would welcome a personal interview at your earliest convenience. Thank you.

Sincerely,

Helen P. Garrett

Enclosure

MICHAEL JENKINS
15 Summerhill Place
Atlanta, Georgia 30966
(404) 702-9675

June 10, 1997

Gene Afseth
Stratus Computer, Inc.
14785 Preston Road, Suite 680
Dallas, TX 75240

Dear Mr. Afseth:

Building profitable technical service and support organizations is what I do best. In fact, for Lackman, I created a service organization that generated over $10 million in annual revenues. Starting with one software support engineer, I created a 115-person, 8-department network supporting more than 1500 customers in the U.S. and Canada.

The experience with Lackman was extraordinary. Not only did I direct the entire service function, I partnered with sales to manage customer presentations, negotiate complex contracts, author customer proposals and facilitate the entire selling transaction. Upon completion, my team and I then took over to direct systems planning, installation and support.

My expertise lies in my ability to recruit talented technical, service and management personnel who are committed to their customers and understand their tremendous impact on revenues, profitability and market retention. Further, I created business processes, standards, systems and milestones to drive organizational change, productivity and efficiency improvement.

After 17 years with Lackman, I resigned my position following a recent IPO. The culture of the corporation has changed, business development has stalled and opportunities are limited. I want to return to a high-growth environment where I can continue to drive change, improvement and financial gain. As such, my interest in your search for a Regional Systems Manager and request for a personal interview.

I'll follow up later this week. Thank you.

Sincerely,

Michael Jenkins

Enclosure

TECHNOLOGY COMPANY MANAGEMENT

KeyWords, Action Verbs & High-Impact Phrases

To "Nail" Your Cover Letter:

* New Technology Development

* New Technology Market Launch

* Revenue & Profit Growth

* IPOs, Joint Ventures & Strategic Partnerships

* Integrated System Solutions

* Competitive Wins

* Capital Financing & Venture Capital/Institutional Investment

* High-Growth Ventures

* International Expansion & Distribution

* Technology Industry Honors & Awards

SABRINA DUNCAN

395 Surrey Place, Flat 2
Avon Von Stratton
London, England
011-34-5-646-8655

May 7, 1997

Carol Holt
Barthoidi & Company
2465 Freetown Drive
Reston, VA 20191

Dear Ms. Holt:

Building corporate and shareholder value is my expertise. Managing within complex technology start-ups and high-growth ventures, I provided the strategic marketing, tactical sales and general management expertise to deliver strong performance. Most notably, I:

- Delivered 300% of profit plan for X-Log Data Systems' operations in the UK in 1996.

- Built X-Log's relationship with British Telecom (one of the top 5 accounts) from $47 million to $100 million in outsourcing and technology sales within two years.

- Captured 160% revenue growth across multiple industries in the US.

- Negotiated strategic customer partnerships with Carnegie Mellon University, Dun & Bradstreet, General Electric, Harvard University, Prudential, Xerox, and numerous other major corporate, multinational and university accounts.

- Spearheaded aggressive, focused and profitable market launch of emerging technologies worldwide.

Currently, I am interested in returning to the U.S. and am exploring senior-level sales, marketing and general management opportunities with a select number of high-growth technology corporations. As such, I would welcome the opportunity to interview for the position of Vice President & General Manager as advertised in The Washington Post.

Sincerely,

Sabrina Duncan

Enclosure

231

MARSHALL WASHINGTON
234 Front Street
Memphis, Tennessee 55441
(554) 564-2893

December 12, 1997

Leonard Stern
Vice President of Operations
ITT Corporation
World Trade Center, 15th Floor
New York, NY 11441

Dear Mr. Stern:

Building corporate value for advanced technology companies is my expertise. Whether challenged to create a complete finance function for a start-up venture, reengineer existing financial operations or provide financial leadership for a fast-track growth company, I have delivered strong and sustainable results. Most notably, I:

- Created a complete finance function for a high-growth Internet company (current employer), transitioning the organization from a $3 million start-up venture into a sophisticated $30+ million corporation poised for dramatic growth in 1997.

- Structured and negotiated large-dollar financings and investments to support the start-up and funding of leading edge technology ventures.

- Reengineered debt management, cash management, accounting and financial reporting functions to strengthen bottom-line financial results.

- Managed relationships with the SEC, NASD and other regulatory bodies.

I am most proud of my success in managing high-profile financing transactions, negotiations and "road show" presentations where my ability to present a favorable corporate profile has been critical. This function alone has been a driving force in the strong operational and financial performance of several technology companies and other commercial ventures. Further, I have an excellent track record in teambuilding, participative management and corporate culture change.

Currently, I am exploring new professional opportunities in advanced technology and would welcome a personal interview with ITT. I appreciate your confidentiality. Thank you.

Sincerely,

Marshall Washington

Enclosure

FRANK JONES
1903 The Highlands
Carmel, CA 93500

Phone: (991) 395-9303

Email: FJones@AOL.com

February 23, 1997

Ronald Madison
Chairman
Dell Computers
1299 Pasadena Avenue
Phoenix, AZ 99841

Dear Mr. Madison:

Recruited to Morris Computers in 1978, I thought I'd spend a few years developing technology and then "move along." Eighteen years later, we had built a $2 billion corporation, recognized as the leader in fault tolerant technology and a pioneer in open systems architecture.

My challenge was to build and lead the technology organization, from its initial foundation of 12 engineers into what is today an 800-person organization with operations in both California and Texas. The tremendous gains in technology and the innovation in systems design and delivery are well documented on the enclosed resume.

Just as significant have been my organizational and general management contributions. It is not often that an individual has the opportunity to shape and build a new organization. Mine has been recognized as the single most critical factor in Morris' success. I have earned a reputation for my ability to build, lead, develop, motivate and retain. In turn, Morris' technology group is one of the most respected in the nation and a true "thorn in the side" of our major competitors. We are <u>always</u> ahead of the rest.

More recently, the president of Morris approached me to lead an aggressive turnaround of a non-performing business unit. Results were equally impressive. We transitioned a $32 million losing operation into what is projected to deliver $25 million in earnings in less than three years.

Recently, Morris has undergone dramatic organizational changes. It is now time to "move on". Thus my interest in meeting with you to explore senior management opportunities. I will follow-up in the next few days. Thank you.

Sincerely,

Frank Jones

Enclosure

GARY R. JORDAN

1934 South Flower Road
Garden City, New York 11737

Residence (516) 544-4087
Business   (516) 791-4747

October 3, 1997

Roger Booker
Booker Executive Recruiters
1200 Park Avenue, Suite 122
New York, NY 10010

Dear Mr. Booker:

The changes in Information Technology are evolving at a unprecedented rate. Never before have we experienced such a phenomenon or so many challenges. As an MIS Director, I am routinely faced with these challenges and the need to evaluate specific technologies and their ability to meet our operating requirements. This is where I have excelled.

During the past 10+ years, I have spearheaded the acquisition and development of emerging technologies to meet current organizational needs while providing the flexibility for change as technologies continue to evolve. Most recently, I directed the integration of object oriented, networking, Internet, multimedia and other technologies that have strengthened internal operating capabilities, reduced costs and improved service levels.

With a unique blend of MIS and general management experience, I have positioned each technology organization as a key partner to the operating management team, responding to their specific needs and recommending proactive systems solutions. In turn, each organization is now recognized as a pioneer in information technologies, respected by their peer organizations and commended for their ability to produce.

Starting my career in the for-profit business sector, I advanced rapidly. Most recently, I transitioned my experience into non-profits, providing them with competitive technologies to drive performance improvement. Now, I am anxious to return to a for-profit corporation where greater opportunities exist for both technological and professional advancement.

If you are working with a client company in need of strong, decisive and proactive MIS leadership, I would welcome the opportunity to explore the position. Be advised that I am open to relocation and that my recent compensation has averaged $145,000 annually. Thank you.

Sincerely,

Gary Jordan

Enclosure

BRUCE GRAPENSTERN

9712 Outback Way
Dallas, Texas 83433-4344
Email: BGRAPE@msn.com

Voice: (815) 530-7179   Fax: (815) 516-9381

August 26, 1997

Mr. Roger Maxwell
President
Nynex Computer Systems
900 South Boston Street
Stamford, CT 09112

Dear Mr. Maxwell:

Throughout my 20-year management career, I have guided software and systems solutions companies through the critical phases of start-up, turnaround and fast-track growth. To each, I have delivered strong and sustainable financial gains:

* 50%+ increase in ROI for STX Corporation.
* 35%+ increase in pre-tax profits for STX's Australian Operations.
* 500% revenue growth for turnkey solutions supplier.
* $10 million revenue gain for one of IBM largest reseller organizations.

My strengths in general management, marketing and business development, combined with my strong technical qualifications, have allowed me to provide quality leadership to each organization. Beginning with a vision, I have created strategic marketing plans, built direct and distributor sales channels, led R&D and product commercialization operations, and dominated major markets in the U.S. and abroad.

Beginning as Marketing Manager for the Australian Region, I was promoted to U.S. Corporate Headquarters in 1994. Since that date, I have reengineered all core business processes for both the Software and Enterprise Storage Divisions, building revenues to over $30 million.

I am confidentially investigating new professional challenges and opportunities and would welcome a personal interview to explore your needs for strong and decisive leadership. Thank you.

Sincerely,

Bruce Grapenstern

Enclosure

235

WAYNE FARRELL
3944 North Star Circle
Topeka, Kansas 65229
(913) 516-9381

September 22, 1997

Chester Taylor
Taylor & Associates
3244 Deer Trail
Boulder, CO 80301

Dear Mr. Taylor:

If you are working with a client company in need of an accomplished technology executive, please consider the following highlights of my professional career:

- More than 15 years of top-flight senior marketing and general management experience (including P&L) with leading high-technology manufacturers.

- Consistent success in building revenues, increasing profits and ROI, reducing R&D and operating costs, and positioning companies for strong and sustainable market growth.

- Leadership of successful start-up ventures, turnaround business units and high-growth corporations.

- Extensive management and business development experience in U.S., Australian and Far Eastern markets.

- Strong technical qualifications and experience with mainframe, UNIX and mid-range technologies, global information networks, numerous operating systems and virtually all leading software packages.

Characterized as "an Australian with a decisive U.S. management style," I built and led U.S. and multinational teams responsible for product development, marketing, sales, technical support, finance, internal MIS, human resources and administration. I am focused in my leadership style and able to make the difficult decisions.

My goal is a top-flight management position with a high-tech corporation, either in the U.S. or abroad, and my compensation requirements are flexible. I appreciate your assistance and look forward to speaking with you.

Sincerely,

Wayne Farrell

Enclosure

ROBERT LEWIS

1093 St. Andrews Lane
Cleveland, Ohio 44052

Residence (513) 459-7410   Office (513) 459-7470

April 2, 1997

Keith Cantrell
President
International Technologies
1201 Stillwatch Way
Orchard Park, NY 14411

Dear Mr. Cantrell:

Throughout my General Management and Executive Sales/Marketing Management career, I have provided the strategic and tactical leadership to accelerate revenue and earnings gains for high-growth, technology-based corporations. Highlights include:

- Between 1995 and 1996, I reignited the growth of WIP Inc., introduced pioneering technologies into new national markets, expanded sales distribution channels, and positioned the company for long-term, sustained earnings.

- Between 1992 and 1995, I delivered 142% revenue growth for Telco Service, introduced nine new technology products to the marketplace, and implemented ACD technology into the corporation to strengthen its order processing and customer service capabilities.

- Between 1990 and 1992, I negotiated strategic partnerships with technology vendors, increased revenues from $97 million to $120 million, and positioned Compuware as the 10th largest IBM reseller in the U.S.

My earlier contributions to Litel Telecommunications and Xerox were equally notable and included significant revenue and market gains. In fact, during my tenure as a Regional Sales Manager with Xerox, I captured over $180 million in new revenues.

My success lies in my ability to identify and capture market opportunity, respond to changing market and customer demands, and exploit the introduction of emerging technologies nationwide. I am direct and decisive in my leadership style, yet flexible in responding to constantly changing markets, economies and competitors.

I was recently recruited from a group of 700+ executive candidates as Vice President of Sales & Support to lead WIP through its next stage of accelerated growth. Unfortunately, it immediately became apparent that the ethics of the organization were totally disparate from mine and I resigned my position within only four months.

Currently, I am exploring new career challenges and opportunities with another technology corporation and would welcome a personal interview. Thank you.

Sincerely,

Robert Lewis

Enclosure

237

TRADING & INVESTMENT

KeyWords, Action Verbs & High-Impact Phrases

To "Nail" Your Cover Letter:

* Fixed & Variable Assets

* Dealmaking & Financial Transactions

* Investment Planning & Analysis

* ROI, ROA & ROE Performance

* Investment Portfolio Management

* Commodities Trading

* International Transactions & Deals

* Corporate Treasury Information Systems

* Regulatory Reporting & Compliance

* Trust Services & Administration

RAFAEL MONTEBON
2987 Southern Drive
Savannah, Georgia 47552

Phone (651) 967-0788

Fax (651) 967-5947

May 16, 1997

Shawn Carrington
Executive Vice President
Bank of New York
1202 Commerce Avenue
New York, NY 10018

Dear Mr. Carrington:

I am a well-qualified, senior-level Treasury and Trading Executive with 19 years' experience in the US, European, Far Eastern and South African markets. Currently, I am exploring new professional opportunities and would welcome the chance to speak with you directly regarding executive positions with Bank of New York.

For the past nine years, I've lived and worked in the US, representing and managing the investment, trading, marketing and risk management affairs of one of the top 100 banks in the world. I've performed extremely well, taking the organization from a loss position to strong profits with a 100% increase in trading volume.

Earlier successes were just as significant:

* Increased trading volume in Japan from $500 million to $6 million with 500% increase in profitability.

* Captured a 150% increase in sales and 300% increase in trading volume in Singapore.

* Established new and profitable South African trading organization.

* Managed $5 billion US treasury and trading operation in France.

Each of these positions has not only required strong financial, investment, negotiating and trading qualifications, but a unique expertise in cross-cultural business development and relationship management. I have established a high-profile reputation within each country and led each organization through change, growth and performance improvement.

I look forward to speaking with you regarding your search for a Treasury Vice President, and appreciate your consideration.

Sincerely,

Rafael Montebon

Enclosure

GILBERT WAINRIGHT

2503 Oak Tree Circle
Yanceyville, New York 14789

Home (914) 259-2820   Fax (914) 254-4047

April 21, 1997

George Robinson
President
Nations Bank
19022 Washington Parkway
Alexandria, VA 22001

Dear Mr. Robinson:

Currently employed as an Assistant Vice President and Senior Trader with Bank of America, I am confidentially exploring new professional opportunities within the investment industry. With the institution for the past 11 years, I have earned an excellent reputation for my ability to anticipate and capitalize upon market performance, leverage market positioning and accelerate profitable yields.

I bring to Nations Bank a unique combination of qualifications with particular expertise in financial futures and options on financial futures. My performance in this particular market has been exceptionally strong and resulted in average annual profits of more than $1.5 million. In addition, I have extensive qualifications in more "traditional" investment products including U.S. Government securities, bonds and mortgage-backed portfolios.

Just as critical to my performance and the success of my investments are my skills in personnel training and leadership, project management, regulatory compliance, market analysis and historical trend analysis. I am decisive in my actions, yet flexible in responding to constantly changing markets, demands and opportunities.

I would welcome the opportunity to meet with you to explore potential trading positions and appreciate your time in reviewing my qualifications. I will follow-up next week to schedule an interview. Thank you.

Respectfully,

Gilbert Wainright

Enclosure

VICTORIA MATHESON
2983 West 22nd Avenue #122
New York, NY 10021

Home (212) 377-8366   Office (212) 237-5492

November 12, 1997

James Peterson
Vice President of Human Resources
Chase Manhattan Bank
2800 Park Avenue, #121
New York, NY 10108

Dear Mr. Peterson:

I am writing and forwarding my resume in anticipation that you may be interested in a candidate with:

- Four years' experience in Trust Services, Administration & Management.
- Nine years' experience in Investment & Portfolio Management.
- Unique expertise in New Client Development & Relationship Management.
- Juris Doctor Degree awarded in 1991 with two years' legal practice experience.

Currently, as an Assistant Vice President with MSXT Deposit & Trust, I independently manage 300+ family trusts for clients in the U.S. and Europe. The scope of my responsibility includes not only the "traditional" functions of trust administration, legal affairs and regulatory compliance, but active leadership of new business development, marketing and relationship management functions to increase our customer base and the value of our trust portfolio. Results of my efforts have been significant and include development of over $19 million in new trust funds over the past 18 months.

My goal is to transition my trust, legal and client development expertise into a new and more challenging environment. Thus my interest in meeting with you to explore such opportunities with Chase Manhattan.

I appreciate your time in reviewing my qualifications and will follow-up with you next week. Thank you.

Sincerely,

Victoria Matheson

Enclosure

FRANK BARTRUM
19 Cherry Tree Lane
Trenton, New Jersey 04770
(201) 648-1428

March 21, 1997

Thomas Richardson
President
Mitchell Investments, Inc.
2140 Sunshine Boulevard
Melbourne, FL 33551

Dear Mr. Richardson:

The time has come, I've sold my snow shovel, and my wife and I are on our way to Florida. This winter proved to be one of the worst and we're headed for warmer climates.

As such, I'm divesting my financial services company in New York and now looking for a position in investment sales/marketing and portfolio management with a Florida-based organization. Highlights of my professional career include:

- Over 15 years of professional experience in financial services, investment management, marketing and portfolio development.

- Unique expertise in index option investment strategies.

- Development of new portfolio to over $20 million in assets under management.

- Negotiation of competitive wins against major competitors.

- Strong skills in investor development and relationship management.

I am currently travelling between New York and Florida on a routine basis, and would welcome the opportunity for a personal interview on my next visit. As such, I will contact you to schedule a convenient time to explore your need for a strong, decisive and well-qualified investment professional.

Thank you.

Sincerely,

Frank Bartrum

Enclosure

JAMES LAWSON

500 Oakmont Court
Lawrence, Illinois 68708

Home   (874) 793-3197
Office   (874) 778-3402

June 2, 1997

Walter Franklin
President
Schwab Investments
2103 Michigan Avenue, #120
Chicago, IL 60600

Dear Mr. Franklin:

Currently Senior Vice President of Government Bond Trading for Wiley Securities, I have transitioned the organization into one of the top-performing trading companies in the market. By controlling our risk, we increased revenues by 42% within just one year while accelerating market share and strengthening our competitive position.

Now, however, I am confidentially exploring new professional opportunities and would welcome a personal interview with Schwab Investments. I bring to your organization a unique blend of qualifications:

- 15+ years' experience in government bond trading, financing and risk management.
- Expert qualifications in team building, training and organizational leadership.
- Proven success in building and retaining client relationships within extremely competitive and volatile investment markets.
- Strong background in systems and process automation.

Throughout my career — with Wiley, E.F. Hutton and Lehman Brothers — I have strengthened the value and performance of each company's government bond trading organization. This value can easily be measured in terms of growth in market share, risk management and financing.

I would welcome a personal interview at your convenience and appreciate your confidentiality. Thank you.

Sincerely,

James Lawson

Enclosure

TRANSPORTATION

KeyWords, Action Verbs & High-Impact Phrases

To "Nail" Your Cover Letter:

* Fleet Management

* Route Planning & Analysis

* Safety Training & Management

* Workforce Planning & Analysis

* Regulatory and DOT Compliance

* Cost Savings & Avoidance

* Insurance & Risk Management

* Vehicle Repair Operations & Preventative Maintenance

* Freight Consolidation & Management

* Logistics Management

JON PAUL FONTBLEU
234 Seaport Drive
Ormond Beach, Florida 32965
E-Mail: jpf@mcimail.com
Phone/Fax: (904) 350-5414

June 14, 1997

Samuel Green
President
Westside Airlines
1200 Commercial Drive, Suite 343
Dallas, TX 78774

Dear Mr. Green:

As Air Safety Consultant to Air France, I am currently leading the initiative to reengineer, expand and strengthen the carrier's emergency response, flight safety and regulatory compliance programs for operations throughout North America and abroad. To date, I have authored several critical planning documents that serve as the foundation for all emergency management functions.

Now, at this point in my career, I am seeking new professional opportunities with a U.S. carrier where I can continue to spearhead flight safety and regulatory compliance affairs.

Unlike many of my peers, I do not practice "reactive" response. Rather, I have aggressively facilitated the development of a "proactive" plan to identify trends, resolve long-standing issues impacting the efficiency of emergency planning teams, and initiate efforts to prevent such incidents. Although experienced in aircraft investigation, my efforts have largely been focused on accident/incident avoidance.

Prior to my career with Air France, I worked for 11 years with an aircraft components service organization, an experience which provided the foundation for my expertise in regulatory affairs, safety and training/development.

A native of France, I am a resident of the U.S. with full working authorization. With an Embry-Riddle Aeronautical University degree in hand (graduated in 1996) and another degree anticipated for 1997, I am now ready for new professional challenges and opportunities. Thus my interest in Westside Airlines and request for a personal interview.

I will follow-up with you next week and do appreciate both your time and consideration. Thank you.

Sincerely,

Jon Paul Fontbleu

Enclosure

GAVIN WRIGHT
259 Court Street
Greenwich, CT 06454

Phone (203) 377-0127
Fax (203) 570-7990

August 2, 1997

Melvin Kreider
President
Kreider Transportation Corp.
3948 Industrial Plaza
San Ramon, CA 98124

Dear Mr. Kreider:

Building corporate value is my general management expertise. By accelerating growth within existing business units, protecting existing revenues and markets from emerging competition, and introducing improved business processes, I have consistently delivered strong financial results:

- As District Manager of AMX America's Western Region Operations, delivered $5+ million in gross revenue growth over a five year period.

- As Marketing Manager for AMX America's Central and Western Regions, reinvented the organization, and rebuilt sales operations from an agency structure into a direct sales organization with strong revenue and profit results.

- As Country Manager for American Lines Limited's overall company operations in Pakistan, increased revenues by more than 12% within a highly competitive international market.

I bring to Kreider broad general management qualifications in strategic planning, finance, budgeting, human resources, MIS and administration. Just as significant is my expertise in international trade, marketing and business development. Most notable, however, is my success in team building across diverse functional lines, management disciplines and cultures.

Currently, AMX America is launching a large reorganization throughout the corporation and I have decided to pursue management opportunities elsewhere. Thus my interest in Kreider and request for a personal interview. Thank you.

Sincerely yours,

Gavin Wright

Enclosure

SPONSOR LETTERS

THOMAS STERN
TECHLABS, INC.
1203 Colonial Lane
Boston, Massachusetts 10221
(501) 554-6321

January 15, 1997

To Whom It May Concern:

You have a great opportunity to hire one of the most talented and most solid finance executives I've ever worked with. Michael Hayden has been a vital support to me, our Board of Directors and our senior operating team for the past 12 years. Without his guidance and financial expertise, Techlab would surely have meet with more difficult times.

Mike's value and contributions can best be summarized as follows:

- His strengths in debt restructuring and management. In sum, Mike has participated, structured and negotiated over $300 million in corporate debt, significantly strengthening our bottom-line performance and improving our market value. His technical financial expertise, combined with solid negotiating skills, were instrumental to these transactions.

- His performance in the design, development and integration of comprehensive accounting functions. As Techlabs has grown and changed in complexion over the past 12 years, Mike has redesigned systems to support our operations, merger and acquisition activities, divestitures and reorganizations.

- His financial leadership of corporate merger and acquisition programs. Mike has provided financial, analytical and negotiations support for more $200 million in projects, working with top-level operating executives throughout each organization. Most significant was his design of an acquisition model which accurately projects financial performance and has been the foundation for many of our development efforts.

On a more personal note, Mike is my ally and my personal confidant. He is trustworthy, discrete and above board in all his actions. He has earned the respect and confidence of the entire executive team and virtually all employees throughout our organization. It is not often that I have met finance professionals able to transcend their analytical nature into a more communicative, people-directed and participative management style. Mike does.

It is with great sadness that I see Mike leave our organization but know that he will thrive in whatever new challenge he accepts. If there is any additional information I can provide, please feel free to contact me directly.

Sincerely,

Thomas Stern, President

DENNIS JAMISON
ARNOLD AERO, INC.
2345 Longwood Avenue
Cedar Rapids, Iowa 66542
(774) 224-2634

September 5, 1997

Philip Caslteton
President
First Union Bank
3000 Main Street
San Francisco, CA 97112

Dear Phil:

You have the opportunity to hire one of the most talented senior executives I've ever had the pleasure of working with.

Rachel Martin is a consummate banking and financial services executive who has successfully met the challenges of unique start-up, turnaround and high-growth institutions. Beginning her career with several of the major players in our industry — Bank of America and Citicorp — her performance was exceptional. In fact, Citicorp selected her to launch the start-up of a new institutional lending organization that within two years has executed over $1 billion in mortgage swaps.

More recently, Rachel has provided executive leadership to several smaller institutions — Empire Corporation of America and Toller Federal Bank. Recruited by Toller's Board of Directors as President and CEO, Rachel was challenged to orchestrate an aggressive turnaround and return to profitability. She not only achieved the Board's objectives, she far surpassed them by:

- Providing a common vision and mission for the entire institution.
- Spearheading innovative, market-driven business development initiatives.
- Divesting non-performing assets and restructuring liabilities.
- Revitalizing market credibility and achieving 100% regulatory compliance.

I know first-hand the power of Rachel's performance and her ability to translate strategy to action to results. She is a dynamic business leader, never daunted by obstacles and always striving to exceed the best of projections. It is with 100% confidence that I encourage you to consider Rachel for any senior-level executive positions requiring aggressive and creative leadership, top-flight marketing expertise, strong financial skills and the ability to build opportunity from challenge.

If you would like to discuss Rachel's capabilities in greater detail, please feel free to contact me. I know that you will be delighted with both her professional competence and her personal demeanor.

Regards,

Dennis Jamison

249

INTERVIEW FOLLOW-UP LETTERS

HAROLD WATSON

1200 Pearl Street
Jamaica, New York 11441
(516) 554-3321

September 26, 1997

Dear Arthur:

To follow-up from our phone conversation regarding your search for a Vice President of Human Resources, I'd like to first of all thank you for your interest in my candidacy. I enjoyed our conversation and believe there may be an excellent "fit" for my qualifications with your client's needs. I'd also like to take this opportunity to highlight a few relevant qualifications.

As a professional, I have designed, developed and managed virtually all core human resources functions. Working from a "hands-on" perspective, my roles have ranged from strategic planning and organizational development to the more "concrete" functions of staffing, compensation, employee relations and more. Experience and contributions are best summarized as follows:

Organizational Development

- Recognized as a pioneer in organizational design, development and improvement, I have spearheaded innovative programs, plans and processes that have consistently improved productivity, efficiency, quality, cost containment and overall performance. Always focusing on maximizing existing resources, acquiring new competencies, developing top performers and facilitating positive organizational change. I am a driver and a team builder, successful in rallying support to achieve organizational, financial and operating goals.

- Within XATAX, I have orchestrated and implemented a series of strategic organizational development initiatives including process mapping, benchmarking, TQM, and aggressive joint venture and partnership programs.

Training & Development

- The cornerstone of my career has been training and development. From 1980 through 1994, although charged with a diversity of HR functions, my principal focus was the design, development and delivery of training programs for technology, manufacturing, engineering and support personnel. My successes include programs that have been implemented widely throughout various corporations including Ameritech, Bell Laboratories, Bellcore, BellSouth, Fujitsu, Siemens and U.S. West. Most significantly, I am recognized as a pioneer in technology-driven training.

- Recently, I was the principal in the design and development of XATAX's first internal MBA program. Not only did I develop overall strategy and training objectives, I also personally authored a majority of the training curriculum, designed instructional tools and actually taught various program components.

Staffing & Recruitment

- I actively participated in the recruitment, interviewing and selection of personnel for multilevel managerial, professional and support positions. Most critical to this function has been the development of appropriate staffing plans and models to maximize labor resources while controlling labor expenses. As a result of team efforts, I have been fortunate to build a number of top-performing organizations recognized for excellence in personnel performance, technical competencies and leadership capabilities.

- During my three-year tenure with Green's German operations, I led the recruitment and staffing affairs to build an international training organization. This included selection of technical, managerial, instructional, administrative and support personnel.

251

Compensation & Benefits

- As a consistently an integral member of management team, I was responsible for the design, development and administration of complete benefit programs and multilevel salary and compensation plans. Inherent in this responsibility are a portfolio of functions   including competitive analysis, market analysis, vendor review, price negotiations, plan design, employee communications and program administration.

- A recent project was the development of a comprehensive benefit and compensation strategy for the entire organization. Working in cooperation with a team of HR, administrative, finance and operating executives, we carved out a new strategy which, upon full implementation, will not only save XATAX significant dollars but provide all employees with improved benefit coverages and competitive salaries.

Employee Relations, Health & Safety

- Building positive and proactive Employee Relations has been one of the most personally rewarding aspects of my career. In each organization, I have positioned myself as an ally to the workforce, maintaining an "open door" policy, driving consistent and positive advances in the cooperation between employees and management. Further created innovative employee communications strategies and programs that facilitate interaction and reward cooperation.

- Throughout my career at Fujitsu, Bell Laboratories and Siemens, I led the design and managed the "hands-on" implementation of a number of employee safety training programs. Each resulted in measurable decreases in employee accidents and workplace incidents.

HRIS Technologies

- For 14 years, I championed the design, development, documentation and delivery of leading-edge training systems technologies for my employers. Created programs which strengthened operating infrastructures, improved staff capabilities and facilitated significant improvements in productivity, quality, efficiency and bottom-line profitability.

- My experience includes a host of other PC applications designed for compensation and benefits administration, employee database management, labor forecasting, manpower analysis and other internal HR functions. Other technology skills are noted on my resume.

Labor Relations & Grievances

- At Bell Laboratories, I was an active participant in the full realm of labor relations, union relations and employee grievances/resolution. I am a decisive management representative who is also sensitive to the needs and expectations of the hourly workforce. This, in turn, has served to strengthen the relationships and cooperation between labor and management to achieve common corporate goals.

Workforce Diversity Management

- I designed and implemented an international workforce diversity training initiative for Health International. This program was critical to the corporation's successful global expansion and diversification initiative, and facilitated the efficient introduction of a multinational workforce.

I trust that the above gives you a more detailed overview of my career and the value I bring to another organization. My goal is a senior-level HR management position that requires hands-on leadership of all employee affairs. I thank you for your time and consideration, and look forward to further pursuing this opportunity.

Sincerely,

Harold Watson

Enclosure

DAVID JOHNSON
1024 Miller Park Avenue
Baltimore, Maryland 22110

Home (410) 757-7981   Fax (410) 754-0430

July 9, 1997

Fortunat F. Mueller-Maerki
Egon Zehnder International
55 East 59th Street
New York, NY 10022

Dear Mr. Mueller-Maerki:

Thank you for this opportunity with Abrams Corporation. Since our first interview, and in anticipation of our second meeting on July 30, I have given considerable thought to the position, the expectations of the European parent company and the challenges inherent in the assignment. To that end, I would like to bring several key points to the forefront.

- I am accustomed to change and growth, a critical factor as outlined in the job description for this position. Most recently, during my tenure as President / CEO of Advantage Corporation, I led the organization through tremendous transition with annual growth of more than 24%.

- My expertise in sales, marketing, new business development and key account management has been a critical foundation for the profitable growth of both Advantage and General Corp. For each, I spearheaded the design and delivery of customer development and management programs that consistently accelerated growth and improved financial performance.

- With 11 years' experience in the plastics industry, I know the market, the players and the competition. This will provide Abrams with a tremendous competitive advantage throughout the Americas market.

- My track record speaks for itself. In each position, I have delivered strong and sustainable results measured in market growth, improved competitive positioning, improved customer satisfaction, and most notably, strengthened revenue and profit growth.

On a more personal note, I have been characterized as a decisive business leader, able to envision, energize and deliver results. Through these efforts, I have earned the respect of all personnel throughout each organization, from the hourly production line worker to other members of the senior executive team. It is this strength in leadership and dedication to performance improvement I bring to Abrams.

I look forward to meeting with you at the end of the month and would be delighted to provide any additional information. Thank you.

Sincerely,

David Johnson

QUINCY ANDERSON
946 Cedar Lane
Nashua, New Hampshire 14532
(619) 554-7512

September 14, 1997

Mr. Steven Wexler
President
Princeton Equity Services
190 Wabash Avenue, Suite 120
Chicago, IL 60661

Dear Steve:

Since leaving our meeting last Thursday, I have thought at great length about our discussion, the tremendous opportunity that appears to be present in the Chicago market, and the value I bring to the organization. As such, I would like to take a moment of your time to address several key points.

First and foremost, I am a "dealmaker" and marketer, able to identify and capture opportunities that have driven strong revenue and asset performance. I tackle each new project with a two-pronged focus: (1) negotiate the best possible transaction that, as trite as it may sound, truly is a "win-win" deal for all partners; and, (2) create strategic and tactical marketing programs that consistently create value, dominance and earnings.

My efforts can easily be measured by gains in the value of real estate holdings and improved project cash flows. Full financial documentation can be disclosed (without conceding the confidentiality of Maxxen Properties). I have maximized the value of each asset under management and transitioned "average" properties into "top" performers. I am driven to succeed and have done so.

You're right. I have never worked directly in the Chicago market. However, I have repeatedly demonstrated my ability to build presence within other new markets nationwide (e.g., Atlanta, Southern California). Further, I have an extensive network of contacts across the country, many of whom are well connected in Chicago and will be of significant value in facilitating the start of my own regional network.

I have always been fortunate in that networking is a natural process for me. I am able to quickly ascertain who it is that I must establish a relationship with, identify the appropriate channels to do so, and quickly begin the process. In turn, despite often unfamiliar territories and personalities, I have quickly established myself in key markets nationwide. I am not daunted by challenge, but rather motivated to succeed and beat the odds.

I hope that you and I have the opportunity to continue our discussions and certainly appreciate the amount of time you spent last week. I guarantee that I can not only meet your expectations, but clearly exceed them.

Sincerely,

Quincy Anderson

Enclosure

BOYD CARY
10293 Cedar Street
New Orlean, Louisiana 78874
(661) 654-8723

September 12, 1997

Charles Taylor
President
PYD Technologies
120 Robert Trent Avenue
Columbia, SC 27104

Dear Charles:

First of all, thank you. I really enjoyed our conversation the other day and am completely enamored with the tremendous success you have bought to PYD. There are but a handful of companies that have experienced such aggressive growth and can predict strong and sustained profitability over the years to come.

I would like to be a part of the PYD team — in whatever capacity you feel most appropriate and of most value. I realize, of course, that you already have an HR Director who has successfully managed the function throughout the course of the company's development. It is not my intention to compete with Leslie Smith, but rather to complement her efforts and bring new HR leadership to the organization.

Let me take a few minutes to highlight what I consider to be my most valuable and substantiative assets:

I have met the challenges of accelerated recruitment:

- In 1993, I launched a recruitment initiative to replace 50% of the total workforce in a 900-person organization. This was accomplished within just six months and was the key driver in that organization's successful repositioning.

- In 1985, when hired as the first-ever HR executive for a growth organization, I created the entire recruitment, selection and placement function. Over the next two years, I hired more than 50 employees to staff all core operating departments.

- Between 1984 and 1986, I spearheaded the recruitment and selection of technical, professional and management personnel. This was a massive effort during which time I interviewed over 300 prospective candidates throughout the U.S. and Europe.

I have met the challenges of employee retention:

- During my employment with Helms Financial, we were staffing at an unprecedented rate. Unfortunately, inherent in this situation is the need to initiate programs to ensure staff retention over long periods of time. The faster an organization grows, the more critical the focus must become. Costs associated with recruitment can be significant and must be controlled. Following implementation of a market based research study, I was able to reduce Helm's turnover 35%, saving over $350,000 in annual costs.

255

I have met the challenges of international human resource leadership:

- Throughout my tenure with Laxton Data, I led the organization's International Employment & Employee Relations function. This was a tremendous experience during which time I developed strong qualifications in both domestic and expatriate recruitment, compensation, benefits administration and relocation. Further, I demonstrated my proficiency in cross-cultural communications and business management. During this period, I traveled extensively and am quite comfortable in diverse situations.

I have met the challenges of growth and organizational change through internal development and acquisition:

- Each of the organizations in which I have been employed have faced unique operating and leadership challenges. These situations have been diverse and included high-growth, turnaround and internal reorganization. Each has focused on improved performance and accelerated market/profit growth through development of its human resources and management competencies. To meet these challenges, I have created innovative, market-driven organizational structures integrating pioneering strategies in competency-based recruitment and performance management.

- Most recently, I orchestrated the workforce integration of two acquisitions into core business operations. This required a comprehensive analysis of staffing requirements, evaluation of the skills and competencies of the acquired employees, and accurate placement throughout the organization. The integration was successful and all personnel are now fully acclimated and at peak performance.

I hope that the above information demonstrates the value I bring to PYD — today and in the future. You will also find that my abilities to lead and motivate are strong and have always been the foundation for my personal success.

I look forward to speaking with you and would welcome the opportunity to meet Mr. Williams. Again, thank you for your time and your interest. I wish you continued success in your efforts.

Sincerely,

Boyd Cary

RALPH EVANSTON

2310 South Howard Drive

Kalamazoo, Michigan 60112

616) 655-3254

September 27, 1997

Dear Mr. Robertson & Mr. Ingles:

First of all, thank you. I have thoroughly enjoyed the time I have spent with you and with your management team. The commitment that each of you has to your employees and, in turn, their commitment to Cantec is remarkably unusual and admirable in this age of constant change and the unfortunate attitude of "each man for himself."

Yes, I want to be part of the Cantec team — in whatever capacity you feel most appropriate and of most value. As an HR professional, my efforts are always focused on the resources and value of the workforce, and what I can do to optimize productivity, build camaraderie, recognize excellence, and create an environment that is both personally and professionally rewarding.

Perhaps the most critical lesson I have learned throughout the years is to "not fix that which is not broken." In this regard, I am referring to the corporate culture that you have already created and which I believe has been the foundation for much of CCR's success. Therefore, it is not my intention to change that which already exists; rather, my goal is to nurture that culture and your employees to even greater heights of performance.

Although we have discussed the following HR issues during our conversations, there are several key points I would like to address:

- <u>2000 employees by year 2000</u>— an aggressive but realistic goal to which I bring significant value. As the first-ever HR executive with Grossman Financial, I created the entire recruitment and selection function, and brought more than 100 employees into the organization. With Lyon, I spearheaded recruitment efforts in both the U.S. and Europe. Most recently, with Baltock, I launched an initiative to recruit 450+ individuals as part of the organization's massive reengineering program. In sum, my recruitment efforts on focused on managerial, technical, professional and administrative talent to meet rapidly changing organizational needs.

- <u>Acquisition integration is also a core issue relevant to Cantec and in which I have significant experience</u>. Knowing the value and success of your organizational culture, it is critical that the individuals retained during acquisitions be promptly, efficiently and completely assimilated into the existing corporate culture, becoming viable and productive team members within a relatively short period of time. I have met this challenge before and will continue to be successful for Cantec.

- <u>International business affairs and expansion</u> Complementing my efforts in domestic HR affairs, I have strong experience in international recruitment, staffing and personnel leadership acquired during my tenure with Lillon. I am sensitive and responsive to cultural differences and successful in using those differences to strengthen the overall competency and performance of the workforce. As CCR continues to grow and expand, this will becoming an increasingly important issue that I can address and appropriately manage.

The goals that CCR has outlined for the immediate and long-range future of the organization require strong HR leadership now. The optimum path is to bring a professional into the organization and allow him/her the time to become part of the team, assimilate into the existing corporate culture, and initiate the plans and actions to achieve organizational goals. I would like to be that individual, responsible for building the leadership and technical talent that will successfully lead the organization into the future.

On a more personal note, the value I bring to CCR is more than just my HR and organizational leadership experience. Just as significant has been my career path which has taken my from the "ground floor" through the ranks to my most recent senior management positions. As a result of these vastly differing experiences, I am able to build camaraderie and trust throughout all levels of an organization. The saying, "I have been there and done that" provides the workforce with a sense of security in my understanding of their needs and my commitment to their success.

I hope that this information is of value to you and further demonstrates my worth to CCR. I look forward to further discussions. Again, thank you each for your time, consideration and support.

Sincerely,

Ralph Evanston

WILLIAM HENDERSON
120 Port Street
Lakeside, Minnesota 55441
(312) 323-5487

Steven Donovan
President
Toshiba International
1209 Marietta Street
Los Angeles, CA 90045

Dear Steve:

Last month's unveiling of Toshiba's new corporate structure clearly indicates that the "dust is beginning to settle" and it's time to get "back to business." Not only do I appreciate your tremendous commitment of time and energy to this project, but also the enormous effort involved in restructuring a management team the caliber of which will lead Sony through its next stage of growth and technology excellence. Congratulations! It's been a lot of work from which I hope you feel both personal and professional satisfaction.

When we last spoke, you indicated there would be an opportunity for me with Toshiba and I'm still anticipating that position. In the interim, I have continued to move my search ahead and am at various interviewing stages with several corporations. Although several of these opportunities are exciting, none offer the potential that is clearly evident with Toshiba. As such, I need your help in clarifying the time frame of my opportunity within the organization.

Let's not reiterate the achievements of my past career. You already know. What I will share with you is what I have learned throughout my career ... that success lies in one's ability to merge the strategic with the tactical, to understand the markets, to know the competition and to build a strong management team. No one function can be accountable for performance. It is the integration of everything and the combined strength of the leadership team.

This is what I bring to Toshiba — the ability to "get my hands around" the entire picture, leverage the opportunities, build the markets and advance technologies.

I thrive in challenging, high-energy and high-performance organizations, much like the "new" Toshiba. Further, I remain highly committed to the challenges and opportunities that await me with Toshiba Pictures Entertainment, and anxiously look forward to your call. Let me assure you that the strength of my leadership experience and track record of profitable performance within the technology industry will indeed be an asset to the new Toshiba management team.

Sincerely,

William Henderson

CHRISTOPHER TUCKER
5 Harmony Way
Bristol, Tennessee 45212

Residence (982) 612-3424   **Business (982) 997-7311**

January 29, 1997

Jean-Yves Dexmier
Chief Financial Officer
Technion Communications Corporation
1001 Murphy Ranch Road
Milpitas, CA 95035-7912

Dear Mr. Dexmier:

When I interviewed with you in December for the Business Unit Controller position with Technion, I was excited. Currently employed with Siemens Communications, I am quite familiar with Technion and its core business lines. Following our discussion regarding Technion's largest technology ventures, I believed that this would be a unique opportunity for us both.

I did, shortly thereafter, speak with Greg Smith who said you were considering promoting from within and that I was no longer a candidate. Now, let me tell you why you should consider my employment.

- **Financial Leadership.** Sixteen years of progressively responsible financial management experience with Sexton Corporation. This includes active participation in the strategic planning, development and leadership of several new finance organizations, much like your current efforts in developing your internal business unit infrastructure. These projects were complex and involved close interaction with the business units and operating executives to develop appropriate analysis, planning and financial processes.

- **Strategic Planning.** Always a member of the strategic planning team, I have not only provided the "numbers" to guide strategic planning and business development efforts, but also championed a number of strategic initiatives. These projects focused on leveraging resources across business units to drive forward strong performance throughout each division and the parent corporation. Further, and perhaps most significant, I am successful in translating plans into tactical action supporting not only the financial organization but each core operating unit.

- **Business Partnerships.** Success in building cooperative relationships and joint partnerships with executive management and operating management teams throughout the Sexton organization. My role as VP of Finance and Controller required constant communications to understand each business unit's operating, financial and strategic objectives. In turn, these partnerships were the catalyst for developing both current financial plans and long-term financial goals. My ability to build these relationships and transcend the image of finance from "watchdog" to proactive business partner has been a key foundation for achievement throughout my career.

- **IS Technology.** Strong qualifications in the evaluation of organizational needs and the selection, acquisition and implementation of advanced information technologies for finance, accounting, administration, operations, purchasing, project management, sales, marketing and much more. In sum, I have facilitated more than $10 million in technology investment including state-of-the-art client/server platforms, decision support systems and enterprise-wide architecture.

260

- **Technical Financial Expertise.** With 20 years of corporate finance experience and an MBA in Finance, I bring to Technion expert technical financial skills. More specifically, I am referring to my competence in financial analysis, financial reporting, financial planning, forecasting, statement preparation, internal audit, internal controls and corporate administration. I know the textbook theory; more importantly, I understand the applications.

- **International Market Experience.** During my tenure with Sexton I was afforded the opportunity to live and work in Germany. This was a particularly rewarding experience after years of working with a multinational workforce. Now I had the opportunity to be part of that workforce. As a result of this experience and many others, I have developed strong cross-cultural and multinational experience, an asset I consider critical in supporting Technion's extensive international customer base.

- **Performance Results.** I have delivered strong operating and financial results in each of my positions, demonstrating my ability to impact positive change and performance. In my current position, I am spear-heading development of a new business unit projected to generate $70 million in first year revenues. Previously, I delivered a 350% increase in productivity for the Audit & Business Controls Division and a $750,000 cost reduction for Rexx Systems in California. Early on, in one of Sexton's other start-up ventures, I co-led the development of a $70 million business unit.

- **Corporate Development.** Participation in mergers, acquisitions, joint ventures and other strategic partnerships as Sexton has grown and diversified its technology interests.

On a more personal note, I consider myself a business professional with expert finance qualifications ... not a pure finance executive. The function has changed dramatically over the years. Today, finance professionals must maintain an active leadership role throughout each business segment. The support and leadership I am able to provide in this role is what distinguishes me from my peers and what will afford Technion a strong competitive advantage.

I hope that you will reconsider my candidacy and allow me the opportunity to again present my qualifications to you and other members of the hiring committee. Your patience, interest and consideration are appreciated.

Sincerely,

Christopher Tucker

FREDERICK RODGERS

18 Quill Avenue
Pebble Beach, Florida 32377
(954) 307-6541

January 23, 1997

Richard Gantsler
Director of Research
Heidrick and Struggles
8000 Towers Crescent Drive
Suite 555
Vienna, VA 22182

Dear Richard:

Thanks for the conversation and preliminary interview. I'm quite interested in the executive sales and marketing position with Marymount Company and would like to aggressively pursue the opportunity. I've been "quietly" searching over the past several months and this is really the first assignment that sparked my interest.

To that end, I wanted to take a few minutes of your time to detail some of my most notable contributions in sales, marketing, customer relationship management and executive sponsorship. I'm sure you'll agree that the depth and performance of my experience can be translated into a significant value-add for Marymount.

As one of only four senior executives with TryxComputers, not only was I responsible for selling and marketing the company, I was also one of the key drivers in the product sales/marketing and customer service/support organizations. Further, I was the corporate sponsor for many key customers and am personally credited with building several of Tryx's largest and most profitable customers — Banamex, Bank of Tokyo, Federal Express, Lucent Technologies, Motorola and SAIC (MIS venture of the NYSE). During my tenure as executive sponsor, Tryx enjoyed the highest revenue per year from these accounts.

My most significant contribution as executive sponsor has been the recapture and resurrection of the Motorola account, now Tryx's largest and most profitable customer account. To understand the impact of this achievement, we have to go back four years when Motorola was in the process of telling Tryx it was going to change vendors (after a four-year relationship). Motorola was in California to present the "loss story" to Tryx executives and Tryx's CEO asked me to join the meeting.

The situation was difficult. The CEO and Senior VP of Sales had attempted an unsuccessful turnaround, yet were determined the keep the account. They gave me the challenge and I produced. I made an immediate (that afternoon) proposal to Motorola based on a new architecture under development and which met all their critical objectives. They travelled to Austin, I listened, they believed and they bought.

Motorola is now Tryx's largest account, generating $70 million in revenues this past year and expected to grow to $100 million within the next few years. Further, I successfully introduced Tryx's newest UNIX technology into the account (currently 50% of total sales and projected to be the majority of system sales going forward).

I can relate similar "success stories" with Federal Express and SAIC, each of which now generates more than $10 million in annual revenues to Tryx. The lead role I played with each of these accounts, and others, has indeed been one of several major contributors to the Tryx "success story."

Let me also bring to your attention that I have substantial experience in Product Management and Product Marketing. As Vice President of the Systems Division, I was directly responsible for product strategy, development and management for much of Tryx's first 10 years (the period of highest growth and profitability).

Over the past two years my focus has been on the aggressive turnaround, market repositioning and accelerated sales growth of the UNIX Division. I transitioned our market focus to the emerging telecommunications industry and established marketing teams to capture key players and channel partners. Results have been strong. The division achieved record sales in 1996 with particular success in the OEM channel (30% over forecast).

Further demonstrating my performance in sales, marketing, negotiating and closing, has been my leadership of several key merger and acquisition projects. Most notably, I was asked to finalize the sale of assets and intellectual property that was being negotiated by the new CEO and another EVP, but had stalled. The deal needed to close prior to the end of the quarter to post positive earnings. Under my leadership, we closed the deal and had a check within 72 hours.

In closing, it is appropriate to point out that one of the keys of good selling is good listening. If you do not understand your clients' needs and expectations, the relationship will never grow and the partnership will never solidify. It is these challenges in product development, customer management and channel development that I have met with strong revenue and profit results.

I welcome your earliest response and again want to thank you for your support.

Sincerely,

Frederick Rodgers

1298 Fletcher's Mill Lane
Kansas City, Missouri 60553
(564) 144-0433

July 1, 1997

Solomon Ritchie
President
Telcox, Inc.
1209 Camino Real
San Diego, CA 93542

Dear Sol:

I've just returned from Mexico City earlier today and wanted to immediately get back in touch with you. I remain very interested and enthusiastic about the CFO position with Telcox, Inc., and believe that the strength of my experience in corporate finance, investor relations and administration will be of significant value to the organization. Knowing that the interest in this position by other well-qualified financial executives is significant, I guarantee that there is no other applicant that will provide the same caliber of decisive leadership.

The task that you face in creating a competitive mindset and culture within the organization is a daunting one. It is with this understanding that I appreciate your need to identify a candidate with extensive experience in corporate governance and financial engineering. In response to those needs, let me note that I have great confidence in my ability to work cooperatively with talented individuals, many with often "strong" personalities.

Further, in my current position, I am spearheading the development of strategic initiatives to drive shareholder value. This effort requires constant communications with the investment community to disseminate information regarding the process and components of our value creation model. Accordingly, I have developed a strong skill set in the intricacies of capital structure, treasury techniques and EVA principles. This, in tandem with my "hands-on" business experience, has allowed me to effectively market our theme throughout the Wall Street community.

I have been characterized by others as an innovator and change agent, constantly striving to enhance corporate value throughout all core business units. I have always been sought out as a sounding board by senior management, a fact that is evidenced by my rapid advancement within the IBM organization. It is this drive and initiative that I bring to Telcox, Inc..

In closing, I wish to thank you for your time, support and consideration. I believe that you and I will be able to build a strong partnership and deliver results critical to the company's long-term success.

I look forward to further discussions on this outstanding opportunity.

Very truly yours,

Marshall Barbour

RESUME & JOB SEARCH RESOURCES

THE ADVANTAGE INC.

Executive Resume & Career Management Center

The Advantage, Inc., one of the nation's foremost resume and job search centers, was founded by Wendy S. Enelow in August 1986. The firm specializes in resume development, job search and career coaching for professional, management, senior management and executive job search candidates. To date, The Advantage has worked with more than 5000 professionals worldwide to plan and manage their successful job search campaigns!

Professional writers and coaches work one-on-one with you to explore your professional goals, develop career strategies, create winning resumes and implement action plans that competitively position you to:

> ## Win in Today's Competitive Job Search Market!

Executive Resume Development	Targeted Direct Mail Campaigns
Cover Letter Writing Services	Internet Online Services
Executive Career Planning & Coaching	Interview Counseling
Executive Job Lead Publications	KeyWord Presentations

Consultations with Wendy Enelow are by scheduled appointment. If you are interested in executive resume, career coaching or job search management services, fax the form below with your resume to (804) 384-4700 or phone (804) 384-4600.

- -

❏ YES!   Please contact me regarding your services and pricing.
            My resume is attached.

NAME: _____

ADDRESS: _____

PHONE: _____

FAX: _____ *Is this a private fax?* **YES**   **NO**

Career Resources

C ontact Impact Publications to receive a free annotated listing of career resources or visit their World Wide Web (Internet) site for a complete listing of over 1500 career resources: *http://www.impactpublications.com.*

The following career resources are available directly from Impact Publications. Complete this form or list the titles, include postage ($5.00 for first book and $1.50 for each additional book) and your name and address, enclose payment, and send your order to:

IMPACT PUBLICATIONS
9104-N Manassas Drive
Manassas Park, VA 20111-5211
Tel. 1-800-361-1055, 703/361-7300 or Fax 703/335-9486

Orders from individuals must be prepaid by check, moneyorder, Visa, MasterCard, American Express, or Discover. We accept telephone, fax, and e-mail orders.

Qty.	TITLES	Price	TOTAL

Author's Books and Audios

Qty.	TITLES	Price	TOTAL
__	100 Winning Resumes For $100,000+ Jobs	$24.95	_____
__	201 Winning Cover Letters For $100,000+ Jobs	$24.95	_____
__	1500 KeyWords For $100,000+ Jobs	$14.95	_____
__	Resume Explosion (audio program)	$29.95	_____
__	Resume Winners From the Pros (May, 1998)	$17.95	_____

Resume, Cover Letter, Interview, Salary Negotiation, & Executive Search Books

Qty.	TITLES	Price	TOTAL
__	101 Best Resumes	$10.95	_____
__	101 Dynamite Answers to Interview Questions	$12.95	_____
__	101 Dynamite Questions to Ask At Your Job Interview	$14.95	_____
__	101 Quick Tips For a Dynamite Resume (June, 1998)	$13.95	_____
__	201 Dynamite Job Search Letters	$19.95	_____
__	America's Top Resumes For America's Top Jobs	$19.95	_____
__	Asher's Bible of Executive Resumes	$29.95	_____
__	Change Your Job, Change Your Life	$17.95	_____
__	Directory of Executive Recruiters 1998	$44.95	_____
__	Dynamite Cover Letters	$14.95	_____
__	Dynamite Networking For Dynamite Jobs	$15.95	_____
__	Dynamite Resumes	$14.95	_____
__	Dynamite Salary Negotiations	$15.95	_____
__	Get More Money on Your Next Job	$14.95	_____
__	Get a Raise in 7 Days or Less (August, 1998)	$14.95	_____
__	High Impact Resumes and Letters	$19.95	_____
__	Internet Resumes	$14.95	_____
__	Interview For Success	$15.95	_____
__	New Rites of Passage at $100,000+	$29.95	_____
__	Resume Catalog	$15.95	_____
__	Resume Shortcuts	$14.95	_____
__	Resumes and Job Search Letters For Transitioning Military Personnel	$17.95	_____
__	Resumes For Re-Entry: A Woman's Handbook	$10.95	_____
__	Sure-Hire Resumes (May, 1998)	$14.95	_____

TOTAL + SHIPPING ($5.00/$1.50) ---------------------- $ _____

http://www:impactpublications.com